EMILY
THE COOKBOOK

EMILY & MATTHEW HYLAND
WITH RICK RODGERS

WITH PHOTOGRAPHS BY EVAN SUNG

BALLANTINE BOOKS
NEW YORK

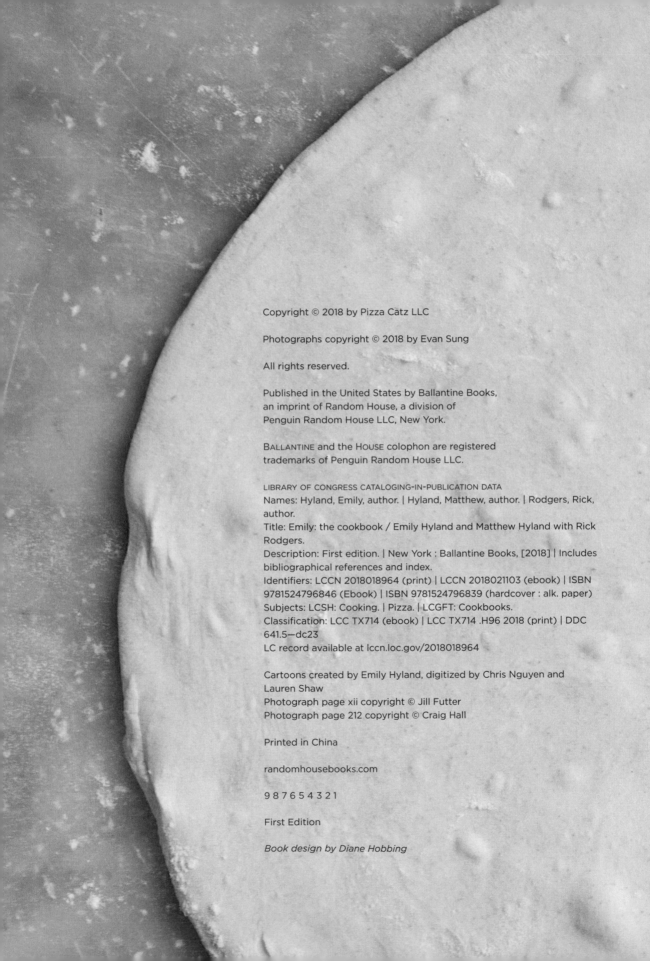

Copyright © 2018 by Pizza Catz LLC

Photographs copyright © 2018 by Evan Sung

All rights reserved.

Published in the United States by Ballantine Books,
an imprint of Random House, a division of
Penguin Random House LLC, New York.

BALLANTINE and the HOUSE colophon are registered
trademarks of Penguin Random House LLC.

LIBRARY OF CONGRESS CATALOGING-IN-PUBLICATION DATA
Names: Hyland, Emily, author. | Hyland, Matthew, author. | Rodgers, Rick,
author.
Title: Emily: the cookbook / Emily Hyland and Matthew Hyland with Rick
Rodgers.
Description: First edition. | New York : Ballantine Books, [2018] | Includes
bibliographical references and index.
Identifiers: LCCN 2018018964 (print) | LCCN 2018021103 (ebook) | ISBN
9781524796846 (Ebook) | ISBN 9781524796839 (hardcover : alk. paper)
Subjects: LCSH: Cooking. | Pizza. | LCGFT: Cookbooks.
Classification: LCC TX714 (ebook) | LCC TX714 .H96 2018 (print) | DDC
641.5—dc23
LC record available at lccn.loc.gov/2018018964

Cartoons created by Emily Hyland, digitized by Chris Nguyen and
Lauren Shaw
Photograph page xii copyright © Jill Futter
Photograph page 212 copyright © Craig Hall

Printed in China

randomhousebooks.com

9 8 7 6 5 4 3 2 1

First Edition

Book design by Diane Hobbing

To Matt:
I choose you, always and forever.
—Emily

To Emily:
Pizza loves you.
—Matt

CONTENTS

INTRODUCTION

Our first shared meal was a pizza. It was pepperoni and olive, eaten while sitting on the floor of Matt's dorm room at school at Roger Williams in Rhode Island. Two days later, on a casual drive to a beach in Newport so Matt could snap shots for his photography class, we stopped for lunch and had more pizza together. A few nights later, Matt took me on a proper date to Al Forno in Providence, a place that was to become a beloved restaurant to us, where we shared their famous grilled pizza. We do eat other food (sometimes), but pizza has been the special fare we have enjoyed sharing since the moment our relationship began.

As soon as we graduated from college, we moved to New York City so Matt could enroll at the Institute of Culinary Education and begin his career as a chef. He has now worked for more than a decade in various restaurants across the city, where he has done everything from making pastry at Public, to smoking meats at the Smoke Joint, to spending his summer slinging pies for Pizza Moto at Brooklyn Flea. When we moved to Brooklyn a few years back, Matt stumbled on our neighborhood pizzeria, Sottocasa, in its opening days. The owner, Luca Arrigoni, invited him to join the founding team to practice the art of making pizza.

Immediately, Matt knew this craft was his path. Luca became Matt's pizza mentor. Within a year, we decided it was time to take a chance and open a restaurant, which was the vision we had shared over a decade before as we ate our very first slices of pizza together. We worked to open our first, short-lived spot, Brooklyn Central, in Park Slope, which turned out to be a stepping-stone for us to emerge onto the pizza scene in New York. After learning some lessons and hitting some speed bumps, we took the opportunity to transition: We searched for a new spot to create a restaurant we could call home in our shared passion for artisanal, high-quality food while still specializing in pizza. It would simply be called EMILY.

While Matt would remain in the kitchen, I would oversee operations in the front and back of the house. If the restaurant was going to bear my name, it was important for me to be as visible as the culinary staff in our small, open kitchen at the back of the dining room. I would set the welcoming tone of EMILY, greeting guests at the door, stopping at the tables to check on the meals, and generally ensuring that the time spent with us would be fun and enjoyable for everyone.

In 2013, our search landed us in Clinton Hill, Brooklyn, a neighborhood that was home to many families and young professionals but had no local eatery. Everything about the location felt right to us. We spent a long autumn rehabbing a previous restaurant space to create a place that spoke of home, comfort, and warmth. This chance we took changed our lives forever. After enjoying the success and crowds at our Brooklyn location, we went on to serve EMILY pizza in the West Village in Manhattan, where we inherited one of the oldest working wood-burning ovens in the city, likely dating back to the late 1800s. After hard work that led to success for our first restaurant, we were blessed with the opportunity to expand, and we opened our sister concept, Emmy Squared, which serves Detroit-style pizza and some killer sandwiches and cocktails in Williamsburg, Brooklyn. After that launch, we opened our first location outside of NYC in early 2018—an Emmy Squared in Nashville.

No matter which location, Brooklyn's Clinton Hill, or Manhattan's West Village, or Nashville, our EMILY philosophy has always been based on the simple joy of eating great food together as well as having friends over for delicious meals in our home. Preparing meals is always about more than the food. It's about the experience of yoking craft and flavor with generosity of spirit. Hospitality, whether in a restaurant or in your home kitchen, is about embracing genuine character.

One of our favorite pastimes is to dine out and spend an evening talking through the nuances of each dish, how the food tastes with the wine we ordered, and how well the meal matches the ambience of the dining room. Matt loves to try new ingredients, see how combinations of flavors work together in unique ways, and find inspiration for playing and experimenting in his own kitchen. Accordingly, much of what he learns finds its way into the meals he makes for others. And we love to cook for others! EMILY is a large-scale version of what we love to do at home: Matt cooks, I host, we serve nice wine and entertain in the coziness of our apartment.

At EMILY, we believe in simple ingredients and simple recipes. Matt's technique is an amplification of flavor. He follows a flavor profile he likes—the richness of dry-aged beef, for instance—adds salt, and suddenly, the funkiness of the meat is alive; he sautés Brussels sprouts with a splash of fish sauce, and suddenly the subtle sprouts are brightened and enriched by the addition. The recipes in this book employ many of the same techniques we use at the restaurant to help simple ingredients sparkle.

Our philosophy is that while food should taste really good, it should also be fun. There are many who preach strict ways of preparing food as either "right" or "wrong." We find this singular way of thinking to be most pronounced in the pizza world: Dough *must* be D.O.C. (that is, *denominazione di origine controllata,* or "designated from controlled origin"). That means it's made according to very strict rules, using *only* Italian flour, water, yeast, and salt, and the tomatoes *must* be San

Marzano. If you are cooking in a Neapolitan oven you *must* make traditional Neapolitan pizza. We take these rules with the proverbial grain of salt. We say, what is "right" is simply what you enjoy. There is no "right" or "wrong" when it comes to pizza. It's all about personal preference. So, cultivate a practice in your kitchen that feels right to *you;* after all, intuition and heart are what the process of cooking is all about.

And while we have become known for pizza and burgers, there are other items on the menu that we hope will really get your appetite going. Our small plates are packed with flavor and have been designed to pass around the table for sharing with others. Our salads are the perfect way to start a meal because they are light; they leave room for the main course. Dessert features decadent and nostalgic options not just from the restaurant but from our moms' recipe collections. And it doesn't matter whether you begin or end your meal with one, just be sure not to skip our house-made cocktails.

Our goal for *EMILY: The Cookbook* is to take you on an in-depth journey on how to make our best dishes and pizzas at home. Although we cook in a professional Pavesi oven in Clinton Hill and a gigantic, wood-burning oven in the West Village, we know you need more practical methods.

Everything we offer in this book is meant to be accessible and approachable, with lots of details to help you along the way. In "Pizza Tools and Ingredients," you'll find everything you need to know to get started. We offer in-depth information on the dough itself, as well as the toppings and various cheeses. Round and Detroit pies are grouped separately in their own chapters, sequenced by the main color of their toppings: red, white, pink, or green. That's how we do it at the restaurant, too.

We reach beyond pizza with our well-known EMMY Burger, providing all of the secrets (it's in the sauce!) to replicate it at home. But our favorite section is perhaps the last chapter with our sauces, condiments, and other extras that you can use in your everyday cooking with recipes outside of this book.

And when it comes to ingredients, a glance through the recipes in this book shows Korean seasoning pastes, Italian bottarga, Indian papadums, Japanese okonomiyaki sauce, Sichuan peppercorns, and many other global influences that inspired Matt. While we give substitutes where possible, there are not always easy swaps. For example, there is no simple substitute for Korean seasoning pastes such as gochujang and ssamjang, which we are crazy about, and we know you will be, too. (The former is one of the main ingredients in the sauce for the renowned EMMY Burger.) We cannot encourage you enough to search out these ingredients. It's more than worth the effort. In almost all cases, they are not perishable and store well for months on end in the fridge so you will have them handy for other recipes. Google them for the best sources, letting your pizza serve as the host for a culinary adventure.

As you cook your way through *EMILY: The Cookbook,* please use it as a guide, not as a rule book. Leave pressure at the door, and take from the book ideas and insights that will make cooking a more enjoyable experience. We encourage you to mix and match—make a dressing into a dip, make a condiment into a drizzle on a pizza—and use our ideas as inspiration for your own pizza inventiveness. Be creative in your approach, trust your instincts, and remember, *never* is there enough ranch dressing to dip your crusts in.

Please keep in touch by taking a photo and tagging us @pizzalovesemily on Instagram so we can see how your homemade pizzas turn out!

With kindness and warmth,

Emily & Matthew Hyland

CHAPTER 1

SMALL PLATES

To start your meal at EMILY, we offer a rotating selection of dishes that will set the stage for the food to come. Knowing that the main courses will no doubt be indulgent, we keep these small plates on the lighter side, and mostly vegetable-driven. We like to offer highly seasonal vegetables when we can to highlight offerings from local purveyors such as Myers Produce or small, emerging greenhouses like Farm One. From our experience eating at lots of pizza restaurants over the years, salads and small plates often feel overlooked or play second-fiddle to the pizza; we prefer to make our best versions of these items to shine just as brightly as everything else on our menu. To help accomplish this, we use unexpected ingredients with a bent toward Matt's affinity for global flavors. And even though some pizza restaurants also have chicken wings on their menu, we wager that they are nothing like our customer favorite, Nguyen's Hot Wings, cloaked in a sticky spicy sauce.

MARINATED OLIVES WITH LEMON AND FENNEL

MAKES 8 SERVINGS

Olives, lemons, and garlic have grown side-by-side for centuries in the Mediterranean region, so it is no surprise that they go so well together. It's worth making a large batch, as they keep for a couple weeks in the fridge. While this method works with other varieties, the Castelvetrano variety, with their mild flavor and plump flesh, is our absolute favorite out of a wide range of olive options.

⅔ cup (165 ml) extra-virgin olive oil, or more as needed

⅔ cup (165 ml) canola oil

3 garlic cloves, crushed under a knife and peeled

1 teaspoon fennel seeds

1 teaspoon black peppercorns

1 bay leaf

3 strips lemon zest, removed with a vegetable peeler, about 3 inches (7.5 cm) long

3 strips lime zest, removed with a vegetable peeler, about 3 inches (7.5 cm) long

1 pound (455 g) Castelvetrano olives

1. Warm the olive oil, canola oil, garlic, fennel seeds, peppercorns, bay leaf, lemon zest, and lime zest in a small saucepan over very low heat until tiny bubbles appear around the garlic and zest strips, 5 to 7 minutes. Remove from the heat and let cool for about 10 minutes. Pour the olives into a large bowl, add the contents of the saucepan, and mix well.

2. Transfer the mixture to a container with a lid. If the oil does not cover the olives, add more olive oil as needed. Cover and refrigerate overnight.

3. To serve, use a slotted spoon to transfer the olives and any clinging ingredients to a serving bowl. Let stand for about 30 minutes, and serve at room temperature. (The olives can be refrigerated for up to 2 weeks.)

SHISHITO PEPPERS WITH SICHUAN OIL AND PECORINO

MAKES 4 TO 6 SERVINGS

Part of the fun of eating shishito peppers is that only one out of ten is really spicy. This phenomenon occurs because the peppers facing the sun while growing turn out to be the spiciest. We play up the heat with a drizzle of our brick-red Sichuan oil and then balance it with the salty sharpness of pecorino Romano cheese and a splash of fish sauce. Cook these outside on the grill for a bit of smoky flavor, or just roast them in a hot oven for similar results.

> 8 ounces (225 g) shishito peppers
> 2 teaspoons canola oil
> 2 teaspoons Sichuan Oil (page 200)
> 2 teaspoons Vietnamese fish sauce, preferably Three Crabs (see below)
> Pecorino Romano in a chunk, for grating

Special equipment: Large handful of oak or maple wood chips

1. Prepare an outdoor grill for indirect grilling over high heat (500ºF/260ºC). Sprinkle the dry wood chips over the coals of a charcoal grill or into the smoker box of a gas grill. (Or position a rack in the center of the oven and preheat the oven to 500ºF/260ºC.)

2. Toss the peppers with the canola oil and spread in a large, heavy skillet, preferably cast iron. When the wood starts smoking, add the skillet to the cooler area of the grill and close the lid. (Or place the skillet in the oven.) Cook, without turning, until the peppers are lightly browned, 7 to 10 minutes.

3. Remove the skillet from the grill (or oven). Drizzle the Sichuan oil and fish sauce over the peppers. Grate a shower of Romano over the peppers to lightly cover them (about 2 tablespoons), and serve immediately, directly from the skillet.

Fish sauce It would be almost impossible to make Southeast Asian food without fish sauce. Called *nuoc mam* in Vietnam and *nam pla* in Thailand, there are also Japanese, Korean, and Indonesian versions. Interestingly, while fish sauce tends to be associated with Asian cuisine, it has been traditionally used in Roman cooking as well; Matt finds it indispensable in most of our pasta dishes, where it works in tandem with tomatoes and cheese to deliver its umami punch. Our favorite is the Viet Huong brand; we also like the Three Crabs variety. Look for the three crustaceans on the label.

SMOKY CARROTS WITH BELUGA LENTILS AND TAHINI DRESSING

MAKES 6 SERVINGS

With bold contrasting colors of orange carrots and black lentils, this dish works well as an appetizer, on a buffet table, or even at a picnic, where it is delicious at ambient temperature. It's best with organic carrots, preferably from the farmer's market, perhaps with a mixture of orange, yellow, and purple rainbow carrots. We love beluga lentils because they offer an al dente texture compared to other lentils and a subtle bed of flavor to the smokiness of the carrots. Like all of our oven-roasted dishes, this one can be cooked on the grill or in the oven.

TAHINI DRESSING

2 tablespoons tahini
1 tablespoon fresh lemon juice
1 or 2 cloves Garlic Confit (page 207), mashed with a fork into a purée
1½ tablespoons water, as needed
Kosher salt and freshly ground black pepper

½ cup (110 g) beluga (also called black or caviar) lentils, sorted for debris, rinsed, and drained
Kosher salt
12 thin carrots (about 1 lb/455 g)
Extra-virgin olive oil
Ground sumac, for serving
Fresh mint sprigs for garnish

Special equipment: Large handful of oak or maple wood chips

1. To make the dressing: Whisk the tahini, lemon juice, and garlic confit in a small bowl. Whisk in enough water to make a thick but pourable dressing. Season to taste with salt and pepper. Set the dressing aside.

2. Put the lentils in a medium saucepan and add enough water to cover by 2 inches (5 cm). Bring to a boil over high heat. Reduce the heat to medium-low. Cook the lentils at a steady simmer, uncovered, until tender, about 30 minutes. During the last few minutes, add 1 teaspoon salt. Drain well and set the lentils aside.

3. Prepare an outdoor grill for indirect grilling over high heat (500ºF/260ºC). (Or position a rack in the center of the oven and preheat the oven to 500ºF/260ºC.)

4. Cut carrots in half lengthwise, and then on a diagonal into chunks about 3 inches (7.5 cm) long. Toss the carrots with 1 tablespoon olive oil on a rimmed baking sheet (or, for grilling, in a shallow disposable aluminum foil pan).

5. Sprinkle the dry wood chips over the coals of a charcoal grill or into the smoker box of a gas grill. Roast the carrots over indirect heat on the grill, with the lid closed, or in the oven, until they are barely tender when pierced with the tip of a small knife, 10 to 15 minutes. Season with salt and pepper. If you wish, cool the carrots to room temperature.

6. Drizzle with olive oil and season to taste with salt and pepper. Divide the lentil mixture among individual single-serving skillets or shallow salad bowls. Arrange the carrots on top and add a dollop of the tahini to each. Sprinkle with the sumac and add another splash of olive oil. Finish each with a mint sprig. Serve warm or at room temperature.

OKI ROASTED BROCCOLI

MAKES 4 TO 6 SERVINGS

This simple roasted broccoli benefits from a punch of flavorful Japanese accents. The amounts for this recipe are loose—we're really talking about drizzles and handfuls instead of precise amounts. Use the measurements for garnishes as guidelines, keeping in mind that you're going for harmony and not one overriding flavor. The oki approach works with other roasted vegetables, too, so feel free to swap something else for the broccoli—we serve roasted delicata squash in this preparation during fall.

> 12 ounces (340 g) broccoli florets, each about 1 inch across
> 2 teaspoons toasted sesame oil
> Kosher salt
> 2 tablespoons Kewpie mayonnaise in its squeeze bottle
> 1 tablespoon okonomiyaki sauce in its squeeze bottle
> 1 teaspoon ground green seaweed (*aonori*)
> 2 heaping tablespoons bonito flakes

Special equipment: Large handful of apple or cherry wood chips

1. Prepare an outdoor grill for indirect grilling over high heat (500ºF/260ºC). Sprinkle the dry wood chips over the coals of a charcoal grill or into the smoker box of a gas grill. (Or position a rack in the center of the oven and preheat the oven to 500ºF/260ºC.)

2. Toss the broccoli with the sesame oil in a large ovenproof skillet, preferably cast iron. Spread the broccoli out in the skillet and grill (or roast) until the broccoli is lightly browned and crisp-tender, about 10 minutes. Season the broccoli lightly with salt.

3. Remove the skillet from the grill (or oven). Squeeze zigzags of the mayonnaise and Okonomiyaki sauce over the broccoli. Sprinkle with the seaweed, followed by the bonito flakes. Serve immediately, as the bonito flakes will twist and turn from the radiated heat, which is part of the fun of eating this dish.

ABOUT JAPANESE INGREDIENTS

At EMILY, we use a plethora of Japanese ingredients. Here are some of our favorites, for which the recipes in this book often call.

Toasted sesame oil is dark and has the distinct aroma of toasted sesame seeds. Avoid the pale yellow domestic sesame oil (usually labeled as expeller-pressed), as it doesn't have the desired nutty taste.

Okonomiyaki sauce is thick and glossy, with a variety of fruits and vegetables to give it a sweet note. It's named for okonomiyaki, a kind of savory pancake that can be filled with just about anything. In fact, *okonomi* translates to "your favorite things" and *yaki* means "grill." The traditional toppings are squiggles of this sauce (which may remind you of a combination of Worcestershire sauce and ketchup) and Kewpie mayonnaise (see below).

Aonori is neon-green seaweed that has been ground into tiny flakes. It is used as a seasoning sprinkled over food.

Bonito flakes (also called *katsuobushi*) are tissue-thin slices of fermented and dried skipjack tuna with an intense marine flavor. They are usually steeped in hot water to make dashi, a classic Japanese broth (but not for our version on page 20). We like to sprinkle the flakes on top of hot foods, where the flakes look like they are coming alive, twisting and turning from the heat waves rising from the food. When purchasing, be sure to choose the larger flakes in large bags and not the smaller packaged ones that are used to make "instant" dashi.

Kewpie mayonnaise is a Japanese brand that is creamier and tangier than American mayo, and it is flavored with both malt and rice wine vinegars. You'll find it at Asian markets in a distinctive clear plastic squeeze bottle with a red flip top.

Kombu is thick, somewhat leathery seaweed that is used to make dashi, the basic cooking stock in Japanese cuisine. It comes in flat sheets that are sometimes dried into crumpled ropes. The powdery white coating on the surface of the kombu is glutamate, which gives the seaweed its special flavor. Do not rinse or wipe off the powder, regardless of conflicting advice in old Japanese cookbooks. (In the past, the seaweed could have dirt or sand clinging to it, but that rarely happens now.) To judge the amount of kombu you'll need, weigh it on a kitchen scale, or use the weight on the package as an estimate. A little more or less won't make much difference.

Dried shiitake mushrooms are used in both Japanese and Chinese cooking. Simmering them in liquid releases their earthy flavor. Use the entire mushroom; don't worry about removing the stems.

Panko is Japanese-style bread crumbs with a crisper, crunchier texture than its American or Italian counterparts. No longer considered a specialty ingredient, panko is sold at supermarkets along with other kinds of bread crumbs.

SEARED BRUSSELS SPROUTS WITH APPLE AND BLACK SESAME SEEDS

MAKES 4 SERVINGS

Brussels sprouts have gone from being an underappreciated vegetable to everyone's favorite in recent years. Searing these earthy little cabbages enhances their natural sweetness, which we pair with apple cubes. A splash of fish sauce and a sprinkle of Romano knits the flavors together.

10 ounces (280 g) Brussels sprouts
2 teaspoons extra-virgin olive oil
Kosher salt and freshly ground black pepper
½ sweet apple, such as Honeycrisp, unpeeled, cored, and cut into ½-inch (12-mm) dice
1 tablespoon Vietnamese fish sauce, preferably Three Crabs
2 tablespoons freshly grated pecorino Romano
½ teaspoon sesame seeds, preferably black, for serving

1. Trim the sprouts' bottoms and cut the sprouts in half lengthwise. Cut larger sprouts in quarters, or they will take too long to cook. Toss the Brussels sprouts with the oil in a large bowl. Season to taste with salt and pepper.

2. Heat a medium, heavy skillet, preferably cast iron, over medium-high heat until the pan is very hot, 3 to 5 minutes. Add the Brussels sprouts, flat sides down, and cook until the undersides are seared, about 3 minutes. Flip them over, cover the skillet, and continue cooking until the sprouts are crisp-tender and charred in spots, about 3 minutes more. (If the sprouts are too hard, remove the skillet from the heat and let stand for a couple of minutes more, covered.) Stir in the apple and fish sauce and remove from the heat. Sprinkle with the Romano, followed by the sesame seeds, and serve immediately, right from the skillet.

SUGAR SNAP PEAS WITH BOTTARGA AND LEMON

MAKES 4 SERVINGS

This super-simple starter illustrates our premise that fine ingredients don't need much preparation to turn them into a memorable dish. We take fresh, sweet sugar snap peas and top them with salty golden bottarga and a dusting of sharp Romano.

> 8 ounces (225 g) sugar snap peas
> ½ ounce (15 g) bottarga, as needed
> ½ ounce (15 g) pecorino Romano, from a chunk, as needed

1. Set up a bowl of ice water. Bring a large saucepan of salted water to a boil over high heat. Add the sugar snap peas and cook just until they are crisp-tender and have turned a slightly brighter shade of green, about 2 minutes. Do not overcook. Drain in a colander and rinse under cold running water. Transfer the drained peas to the ice water and let cool completely, about 5 minutes. Drain well and pat dry with paper towels.

2. Cut the peas crosswise on a diagonal into ⅛-inch (3-mm) strips. Spread the peas on a serving platter. Using a Microplane, grate a light, even topping of bottarga over the peas. Repeat with the Romano. Serve immediately.

Bottarga Around the world, you'll find salted and cured fish roe. The Italian version, bottarga, comes from the Italian islands of Sicily and Sardinia. Because cattle and their milk are not abundant in those regions, dried fish roe stands in as a substitute for such salty, hard, grating cheeses as Parmigiano, pecorino Romano, and grana padano.

In Sicily, bottarga is made from tuna roe (*tonno*), and in Sardinia, gray mullet (*muggine*) gets the honor. You'll find vacuum-packed bottarga in well-stocked Italian specialty foods stores. We prefer the mullet version. Bottarga is often coated in wax to seal it for shipping. If yours has been packed that way, peel away the coating before using.

Even after opening, bottarga will keep for months stored in a ziplock plastic bag in the refrigerator. To use it, finely grate the bottarga on a Microplane so its tiny golden-to-amber-colored shreds will fall directly onto the food. Try it tossed with hot spaghetti and a squeeze of lemon for a super-easy supper.

NGUYEN'S HOT WINGS WITH RANCH DIP

MAKES 4 TO 6 SERVINGS

Be sure not to lose one drop of the sticky and spicy sauce clinging to these wings. At the restaurant, we give them a quick turn in the deep fryer to give their exterior an extra layer of crispness. However, at home you can just roast the wings and skip the frying step. In any case, provide lots of napkins—you'll need them.

> **12 whole chicken wings, about 5 pounds (2.3 kg)**
> **1 teaspoon kosher salt**
> **Canola oil, for deep-frying**
> **Nguyen Sauce (page 198)**
> **Sesame seeds, for garnish**
> **Radishes, preferably French breakfast, for garnish**
> **½ cup (120 ml) Chive Ranch Dressing (page 199), for serving**

1. Position a rack in the center of the oven and preheat the oven to 425ºF (220ºC). Line a large rimmed baking sheet (half-sheet pan) with parchment paper. (This helps keep the chicken wings from sticking to the pan and tearing the skin.)

2. Season the wings all over with the salt. Spread on the prepared pan, skin side up. Roast, turning the wings halfway during cooking, until they are golden brown and show no sign of pink when pierced at the elbow joint, 50 to 55 minutes. (If you wish, the chicken wings can be served at this point. Skip the next three steps.)

3. Let the wings cool completely. Cover with aluminum foil and refrigerate until chilled, at least 4 hours or up to 1 day.

4. To serve, pour enough oil into a large, wide, and deep saucepan to come about 2 inches (5 cm) up the sides and heat over high heat to 365ºF (185ºC) on a deep-frying thermometer. Preheat the oven to 200ºF (95ºC). Place a large wire rack on a large rimmed baking sheet (half-sheet pan).

5. In batches, taking care that the oil does not boil over, add the wings to the oil, and deep-fry until they are crisp and a shade darker, about 2 minutes. Using a wire spider or tongs, transfer the wings to the rack and keep warm in the oven until they have all been fried.

6. Put the wings into a large bowl and drizzle with the Nguyen sauce. Using kitchen tongs, toss the wings in the sauce, being sure not to break them apart. Transfer them to a platter. Sprinkle with the sesame seeds. Serve hot, with the sliced radishes and small bowls of the ranch dressing on the side for dipping.

FIVE-SPICE DUCK RILLETTES

MAKES 6 TO 8 SERVINGS

Rillettes is a variation of confit, the French specialty of poultry (or pork) cooked in its own fat. The chunky spread is slathered on a sliced baguette and served with puckery pickles and sharp mustard to cut through the richness. Homemade five-spice powder gives these rillettes a Chinese flavor that is entirely in step with the traditional version. Though fairly easy to make, you'll need some time: Start three days ahead of serving to cure the duck and age the rillettes. The refrigerated rillettes, thanks to being cured and sealed with duck fat, will keep for a couple of weeks.

FIVE-SPICE CURING MIXTURE
2 star anise pods, broken into points (14 to 16 points total)
1 teaspoon Sichuan peppercorns
¾ teaspoon black peppercorns
¾ teaspoon whole cloves
½ teaspoon ground cinnamon
2½ teaspoons kosher salt
1 teaspoon sugar

RILLETTES
4 duck leg quarters (about 2 pounds/910 g)
1 cup (240 ml) rendered duck fat, melted and warm
1 star anise pod

¼ cup (60 ml) Dijon mustard
¼ cup (60 ml) stone-ground mustard
Baguette slices, for serving
Cornichons, for serving

1. To make the curing mixture: Grind the star anise, Sichuan and black peppercorns, and cloves together in an electric spice or coffee grinder. Add the cinnamon and pulse to combine the spices. Set aside ½ teaspoon of the five-spice mixture in a small jar or bowl and cover tightly. Transfer the remaining spices to a small bowl, add the salt and sugar, and mix well.

2. Place the duck in a baking dish large enough to hold it snugly. Season the duck all over with the curing mixture, rubbing it in with your fingers. Be sure all of the mixture is on the duck. Place the duck, skin side up, on a wire rack set over a rimmed baking sheet. Refrigerate, uncovered, for at least 18 or up to 24 hours.

3. Position a rack in the center of the oven and preheat the oven to 350°F (180°C). Quickly rinse the duck under cold running water and wipe off most of the curing mixture with paper towels—some of it can remain on the skin. Place the duck, skin side down, in a baking dish large enough to hold it snugly. Bake, uncovered, until there is a visible layer of rendered duck fat in the dish, about 30 minutes. Remove the dish from the oven. Turn the duck over, skin side up, and pour in the duck fat. Cover the dish tightly with aluminum foil. Return to the oven. Reduce the oven temperature to 300ºF (150ºC). Continue baking until the duck is very tender, about 1½ hours. Remove from the oven, uncover, and let stand until easy to handle and still warm, about 45 minutes.

4. Discard the duck skin, bones, and gristle, reserving the meat. Strain the duck fat in the baking dish through a wire sieve over a bowl and reserve the fat.

5. Tear the meat with your fingers into bite-sized chunks. Transfer half of the duck to the bowl of a standing heavy-duty mixer fitted with the paddle attachment. Mix on medium-low speed, gradually adding ¼ cup (60 ml) of the melted duck fat, until the meat is shredded and the mixture looks somewhat pasty. Add the reserved duck meat and 3 tablespoons of the duck fat and mix just until combined. Taste the rillettes and season to taste with salt and the reserved five-spice mixture. Pack the rillettes firmly in a serving bowl with about 2 cups' (480 ml) capacity, leaving some headroom. Pour the remaining strained duck fat over the top of the rillettes. Place the star anise pod on top. Refrigerate until the duck fat is solid and the flavors meld, at least 18 hours. The rillettes can be covered tightly with plastic wrap and refrigerated for up to 2 weeks.

6. Remove the rillettes from the refrigerator about 1 hour before serving to lose its chill. To serve, mix the Dijon and stone-ground mustards together in a small bowl. Serve the rillettes with the baguette slices for spreading, with the mustard mixture and cornichons on the side.

Sichuan peppercorns are sold in bags at Chinese grocers. Dark brick-red in color, they are the dried berries of a bush and are not related to black, white, or green peppercorns (which grow on vines). They are not really hot or spicy, but they do deliver a slight numbing sensation when eaten, which is not quite the same as the heat from conventional peppers or chiles.

BEEF MEATBALLS WITH RICOTTA AND BASIL

MAKES 6 TO 8 SERVINGS

We offer these meatballs topped with fresh ricotta as a recurring special at EMILY. There's no salt in the recipe because sufficient seasoning is provided by the fish sauce, Worcestershire sauce, and Romano. This makes 24 nicely-sized meatballs.

MEATBALLS

Canola oil, for the broiler pan

1½ pounds (680 g) ground beef chuck

2 cups (225 g) dried plain bread crumbs

2 large eggs, beaten

½ cup (25 g) finely chopped fresh flat-leaf parsley leaves

¼ cup (60 ml) whole milk

2 tablespoons Vietnamese fish sauce, preferably Three Crabs

2 tablespoons Worcestershire sauce

3 tablespoons freshly grated pecorino Romano

3 tablespoons minced garlic

½ teaspoon freshly ground black pepper

Red Sauce (page 48)

½ cup (115 g) ricotta, preferably Fresh Ricotta (page 208), as needed for serving

Handful of fresh large basil leaves, for serving

Extra-virgin olive oil, for serving

1. To make the meatballs: Lightly oil a broiler pan. Crumble the ground beef into a large bowl. Add the bread crumbs, eggs, parsley, milk, fish sauce, Worcestershire sauce, Romano, garlic, and pepper. Using your hands, mix well, but do not compact the mixture or the meatballs will be tough. Using about 3 tablespoons per meatball, shape into 24 equal balls and transfer to the prepared broiler pan.

2. Position the broiler rack about 6 inches (15 cm) away from the heat source and preheat the broiler on high.

3. Broil the meatballs, turning once or twice, until browned and cooked through, about 10 minutes. If the meatballs are browning too quickly, move them farther away from the heat source.

4. For each serving, place 3 meatballs in a flameproof soup bowl or single-serving skillet. Top with a spoonful of red sauce, and add a generous dollop of ricotta. Return to the broiler and heat until the ricotta melts, about 30 seconds. Top each with a fresh basil leaf, drizzle with oil, and serve.

CREMINI MUSHROOM ARANCINI

Arancini means "oranges" in Italian, which these golden breaded balls, filled with cremini risotto, resemble in size. Sometimes they are called *suppli al telefono* ("telephone wires") because of the way the cheese can stretch into a long line when you eat them. About the only thing Italian in these is their name, because we cook the rice with a Japanese dashi cooking stock. Call them what you want—they are outrageously good.

VEGETARIAN DASHI

2 ounces (60 g) kombu, cut with scissors into large pieces roughly
    3 inches (7.5 cm) square
8 dried shiitake mushrooms

RICE

2 tablespoons extra-virgin olive oil
6 ounces (170 g) fresh cremini mushrooms, stemmed and cut into
    ½-inch (12 mm) or smaller dice
1 cup (215 g) Arborio rice
2 tablespoons puréed Garlic Confit (page 207)
2 teaspoons Vietnamese fish sauce, preferably Three Crabs, or soy sauce
Vegetarian Dashi (above)
½ cup (50 g) shredded Havarti cheese
⅓ cup (40 g) freshly grated pecorino Romano cheese
Freshly ground black pepper

ARANCINI

Rice (above)
3 ounces (85 g) fresh mozzarella, cut into twelve ½-inch (12-mm) chunks
    (you can piece together any trimmings)
1 cup (130 g) unbleached all-purpose flour
3 large eggs
1½ cups (105 g) panko
Vegetable oil, for deep-frying
Okonomiyaki sauce, for dipping

1. To make the dashi: Bring 2 quarts (2 L) water and the kombu to a boil in a medium saucepan over high heat. Reduce the heat to low and simmer for about 10 minutes. Remove and discard the kombu, pressing out the cooking liquid back into the saucepan. Add the dried shiitakes and return to a simmer over high heat. Reduce the heat to low again and simmer until the dashi is fully flavored, about 30 minutes. Strain the dashi through a fine wire sieve, leaving any grit in the bottom of the bowl. Rinse out the saucepan and return the dashi to it. Place over very low heat to keep the dashi warm but not simmering.

2. To make the rice: Heat the oil in a large, heavy saucepan over medium-high heat. Add the fresh creminis and cook, stirring often, until they begin to brown, about 6 minutes. Stir in the rice, garlic confit, and fish sauce. Add about ¾ cup (180 ml) of the warm dashi and cook, adjusting the heat to keep the rice mixture at a steady simmer and stirring almost constantly to avoid sticking, until the rice has absorbed most of the liquid, about 2 minutes. Repeat the process, adding more dashi and stirring until it is almost completely absorbed and the rice is tender, about 20 minutes. (The mixture should be very thick at this point, with very little cooking liquid.) You might not use all of the dashi, which can be cooled, covered, and refrigerated for another use. On the other hand, if you run out of dashi, use hot water. Remove from the heat and stir in the Havarti and Romano cheeses. Transfer to a large bowl and let cool until tepid. Season to taste with pepper (you might not need any salt).

3. Line a baking sheet with parchment or wax paper. Shape the rice mixture into 12 plum-sized balls. One at a time, using your forefinger, poke a hole in the center of a ball, insert a mozzarella cube, and close up the rice to cover the cube. Set the ball on the prepared baking sheet. Cover the balls and refrigerate until chilled and firm, at least 2 hours or up to 4 hours.

4. Put the flour in a shallow bowl. Beat the eggs until combined in a second bowl. Put the panko in a third bowl. One at a time, roll a rice ball in the flour to coat, then in the eggs, and finally in the panko. Return to the baking sheet.

5. Position a rack in the center of the oven and preheat the oven to 200ºF (95ºC). Line a small rimmed baking sheet (quarter-sheet pan) with a wire rack.

6. Pour enough oil to come about halfway up the sides of a large, heavy, wide saucepan. Heat over high heat until the oil reads 350ºF (180ºC) on a deep-frying thermometer. In batches, without crowding, carefully add the balls to the oil (the oil will bubble up but take care that the oil does not boil over) and deep-fry, turning as needed, until the arancini are golden brown, about 3 minutes. Using a wire spider or a slotted spoon, transfer the balls to the paper towels to briefly cool and drain. Transfer to a serving platter.

7. Serve immediately, with the okonomiyaki sauce for dipping.

CHAPTER 2

SALADS AND DRESSINGS

Pizza and salad complement each other so well, and we always have a selection of seasonal favorites on the menu. One of our house favorites is our Brussels sprouts salad, which is especially good in the winter months when tender greens aren't readily available. Summer's bounty is represented by a salad that showcases two favorites, sweet and juicy watermelon and farm-fresh heirloom tomatoes, combined with an olive oil vinaigrette. Our take on Caesar salad showcases mild white anchovies and crunchy Indian papadums among tender leaves of Baby Gem lettuce. Our salads bring a super-fresh element to the table, so serve them immediately after making. Some of these dressings are perfect for tossing with just about any combination of greens and vegetables for a weeknight salad. Do as we do at home, and make large batches of dressing to have on hand when your salad deserves something a little more special than the standard vinaigrette.

BABY GEM CAESAR SALAD WITH DRAGONCELLO VINAIGRETTE

MAKES 4 SERVINGS

Our version of Caesar salad is much lighter than the kind you may be used to. Baby Gem lettuce has small, tender leaves, similar to romaine hearts, which can be substituted. *Dragoncello* (Italian for "tarragon") vinaigrette adds anchovy and garlic flavors. For the toppings, thin Indian papadums and mild white anchovies are our swaps for chunky croutons and pungent brown anchovies.

DRAGONCELLO VINAIGRETTE

1 large egg

2 teaspoons nonpareil capers, rinsed under cold water and drained

Canola oil, for frying

2 teaspoons coarsely chopped Garlic Confit (page 207)

2 teaspoons drained and minced brown anchovies in oil, or 2 teaspoons anchovy paste

¼ cup (60 ml) unseasoned rice wine vinegar

½ teaspoon Dijon mustard

½ teaspoon stone-ground mustard

⅓ cup (75 ml) plus 1 tablespoon extra-virgin olive oil

2 tablespoons Garlic Oil (page 207)

1 tablespoon chopped fresh tarragon

Kosher salt and freshly ground black pepper

SALAD

4 papadums, preferably plain

4 small heads Baby Gem lettuce, separated into individual leaves

⅓ cup (75 ml) Dragoncello Vinaigrette (above), as needed

16 white anchovy fillets

1. To make the vinaigrette: Put the egg in a small saucepan and add enough cold water to cover by ¼ inch (6 mm). Bring to a full boil over high heat. (Large bubbles will appear under the egg and start to move it around.) Remove from the heat and cover tightly. Let stand for 15 minutes. Using a slotted spoon, transfer the egg to a bowl of ice water and let stand to chill while preparing the dressing. Be sure to chill the egg well.

2. Pat the capers dry with paper towels. Pour enough oil to come ½ inch (12 mm) up the sides of a small saucepan. Heat over high heat until the oil is shimmering. Add the capers and fry until they "blossom," 15 to 30 seconds. Using a wire spider or fine-mesh wire sieve, transfer the capers to paper towels to drain and cool.

3. Crack the egg all over and peel, starting at the large end. Slice the egg in half, separate the yolk from the white, and coarsely chop the yolk. Reserve the white for another use.

4. Finely chop the garlic confit, brown anchovies, and capers. Whisk the vinegar and mustards in a medium bowl and whisk well. Gradually whisk in the olive and garlic oils. Add the yolk, garlic confit mixture, and tarragon and mix without breaking up the yolk—the vinaigrette should have a bit of texture. Season to taste with salt and pepper. Transfer to a lidded container. Cover and refrigerate for up to 3 days. Makes about 1 cup (240 ml).

5. To make the salad: Heat a large, dry skillet over high heat. One at a time, add a papadum and cook, pressing occasionally so it comes into even contact with the skillet surface, turning once, until lightly toasted and dotted with small bubbles, about 2 minutes. Transfer the papadum to a baking sheet and let cool completely.

6. Gently toss the lettuce and dressing in a large bowl, adjusting the amount of dressing to your taste. Place each papadum on a dinner plate. Divide the leaves among the plates, stacking them loosely on the papadum. Top each salad with 4 white anchovy fillets and serve immediately.

White anchovies Every supermarket carries brown anchovy fillets in tins or jars. Either you appreciate these salty little slivers of fishy flavor or you don't. White anchovy fillets are different from the brown ones in almost every way. Hailing from Spain (where they are called *boquerones* and are popular as an ingredient in tapas) or Italy, white anchovies are larger, with tender flesh and silver-white skin, and are typically marinated in olive oil and vinegar. White anchovies are usually sold from the display case in Mediterranean delicatessens, but if you search, you might find them in the refrigerated section of specialty markets.

Papadums These snacks, sold at Indian markets, look like thin tortillas flecked with spices. There are many regional variations, made with lentil, chickpea, or rice flour, and seasoned with black pepper, garlic, mixed spices, and everything in between. For a neutral flavor, we use the plain papadums, but don't be too choosy, because you could be pleasantly surprised with other kinds. Note that they need to be cooked before serving!

CUCUMBER, FAVA BEAN, AND CHICKPEA SALAD WITH CURRIED YOGURT DRESSING

MAKES 4 SERVINGS

Here is a substantial salad without a single green leaf. Instead, crisp cucumbers and firm beans are combined and served in a pool of tangy spiced-yogurt dressing.

CURRIED YOGURT DRESSING
½ cup (120 ml) whole milk or low-fat (not nonfat) Greek yogurt
1 tablespoon Thai yellow curry powder
1 teaspoon honey
½ teaspoon kosher salt
2 to 3 tablespoons water

SALAD
2 Persian cucumbers, scrubbed but unpeeled, halved lengthwise, and
    cut into ½-inch (12-mm) chunks
1½ cups (225 g) cooked fresh or thawed fava beans, peeled (see below)
1½ cups (245 g) cooked chickpeas (see page 29)
½ small red onion, coarsely chopped
2 tablespoons extra-virgin olive oil, plus more for serving
Kosher salt and freshly ground black pepper
Curried Yogurt Dressing (above)

1. To make the dressing: Whisk the yogurt, curry, honey, and salt in a small bowl. Whisk in enough water to make a thick but pourable dressing. (The dressing can be covered and refrigerated for up to 2 days.)

2. To make the salad: Toss the cucumbers, fava beans, chickpeas, red onion, and the 2 tablespoons olive oil in a medium bowl. Season to taste with salt and pepper.

3. Divide the dressing among four dinner plates and spread each portion into a pool. Top with the cucumber mixture. Drizzle with oil and serve immediately.

Fava beans To use fresh fava beans, shuck about 1½ pounds (680 g) fava bean pods to yield 1½ cups (225 g) beans. Bring a large saucepan of salted water to a boil over high heat. Add the beans and cook to loosen their skins, about 1 minute. Using a wire spider or sieve, transfer the beans to a bowl of ice water. Reduce the heat under the saucepan to medium-low to keep the water simmering. Let the beans stand for 1 minute. Drain well. Peel the beans. Set up a fresh bowl of ice water. Return the beans to the simmering water and cook just until tender, about 2 minutes (or a bit longer for larger beans). Using the spider, transfer the cooked beans to the ice water, drain, and pat dry.

BIBB SALAD WITH CRISPY CHICKPEAS AND TRUFFLE-HONEY MUSTARD DRESSING

MAKES 4 SERVINGS

The folks at Gotham Greens are our friends, neighbors, and purveyors of the leafy produce for the restaurant. They supply us with the beautifully tender Bibb lettuce that we use for this signature salad. Be sure to refrigerate the chickpeas overnight to dry them in advance of frying, for a crispy deep-fried exterior.

TRUFFLE-HONEY MUSTARD DRESSING

⅓ cup (75 ml) plus 1 tablespoon truffle mustard, preferably Truffleist
  (or 3 tablespoons *each* stone-ground mustard and Dijon mustard)
2 tablespoons truffle honey, preferably Truffleist
1 tablespoon yuzu juice or fresh lime juice
1 tablespoon fresh lemon juice
1 teaspoon kosher salt
3 tablespoons canola or grapeseed oil
2 tablespoons extra-virgin olive oil, or 1 tablespoon extra-virgin olive oil
  and 1 tablespoon white truffle oil, preferably Truffleist

CRISPY CHICKPEAS

1 cup (165 g) cooked chickpeas (see page 29)
Vegetable oil, for deep-frying
Kosher salt

SALAD

2 heads Bibb lettuce, separated into leaves
½ cup (120 ml) Truffle-Honey Mustard Dressing (above)
Crispy Chickpeas (above)
2 radishes, preferably breakfast radishes, ends trimmed, thinly sliced on
  a mandoline or V-slicer

1. To make the dressing: Whisk the mustard, honey, yuzu juice, lemon juice, and salt together in a medium bowl. Gradually whisk in the canola and olive oils. Transfer to a lidded container. (The dressing can be refrigerated for up to 5 days. Whisk well before serving.) Makes about 1⅓ cups (315 ml).

2. To make the crispy chickpeas: At least 8 hours before serving, spread the chickpeas in a single layer on a small rimmed baking sheet (quarter-sheet pan) or plate. Refrigerate uncovered to dry their surfaces, at least 8 or up to 24 hours.

3. Pour enough oil to come 2 inches (5 cm) up the side of a medium, heavy saucepan and heat over high heat to 350ºF (180ºC) on a deep-frying thermometer. In two batches, deep-fry the chickpeas until they are golden brown and crispy, about

2 minutes. Using a wire spider or a slotted spoon, transfer the chickpeas to paper towels to drain. Let the oil reheat between batches. Season the warm chickpeas with salt to taste. Transfer them to a plate. They can be stored, uncovered, at room temperature for up to 8 hours.

4. To make the salad: Gently toss the lettuce with the dressing in a large bowl—the leaves are tender, and you want them to retain their shape, so be careful. Arrange the leaves in a concentric pattern in a wide serving bowl, with the larger leaves on the outside—the idea is for the leaves to look like a large head of lettuce. Sprinkle with the chickpeas and add the radishes. Serve immediately.

COOKING CHICKPEAS

Chickpeas, also called garbanzo beans, require an overnight soak in water—a good start to get them tender. Our favorite method for cooking is the old-fashioned stovetop technique. Use at least 1 cup (200 g) of dried chickpeas and save any leftover cooked beans for another meal. Sort through the dried beans for stones and debris, then rinse them well in a colander under cold running water. Put them in a large bowl and add at least 2 inches (5 cm) cold water to cover. The beans will swell to at least double their size, so don't skimp on the water. Soak at room temperature (or, if the kitchen is hot, in the fridge) for at least 4 hours or overnight. Drain well. Transfer the chickpeas to a large saucepan and add enough fresh water to cover them by 2 inches (5 cm). Bring to a boil over high heat. Reduce the heat to medium-low. Cook the chickpeas at a steady simmer, uncovered, for 45 minutes. Stir in 2 teaspoons kosher salt (or enough to give the water a noticeably, but not overwhelmingly, salty taste) and simmer until the beans are tender, about 30 minutes longer. If the water goes below the level of the beans, add boiling water to keep them covered. Don't be surprised if the beans take longer than this to cook. Drain the beans in a colander, rinse under cold running water to stop the cooking, and drain again. One cup of dried chickpeas yields about 3 cups (495 g) cooked. They can be refrigerated in a covered container for up to 5 days, or frozen for up to 3 months.

Yuzu juice A member of the citrus family, with its thick, bumpy skin and seedy flesh; the fruit's tart juice is prized by many chefs and it is an important ingredient in ponzu, a dip for sushi. It is rare to find fresh yuzu in America, so purchase the bottled yuzu juice sold in small green bottles at Japanese markets.

Truffle products Our friend Jimmy Kunz produces the Truffleist line of handcrafted, small-batch foods, and we love to support him. His mustard and honey are two of our favorites, and we use them in this flavor-packed dressing.

SHREDDED BRUSSELS SPROUTS WITH BLUE CHEESE, BACON, AND MISO DRESSING

MAKES 4 TO 6 SERVINGS

Shredded Brussels sprouts have a firm texture and robust flavor that can stand up to this relatively thick miso and sweet soy dressing. Sometimes we serve this with chopped roasted cashews instead of the pecan halves, and in that case, the nuts don't need to be toasted. The salad is a wonderful one for entertaining because it works just as well as a buffet dish as for a first course.

MISO AND SWEET SOY DRESSING

1 cup (240 ml) store-bought mayonnaise, preferably Hellmann's or Kewpie
2½ tablespoons red (*aka*) miso
2½ tablespoons sweet soy sauce

SALAD

⅓ cup (40 g) pecan halves
2 strips thick-cut bacon
1 pound (455 g) Brussels sprouts, ends trimmed
½ cup (120 ml) Miso and Sweet Soy Dressing (above), as needed
⅓ cup (40 g) crumbled blue cheese

1. To make the dressing: Whisk all of the ingredients together in a medium bowl. Transfer to a lidded container. Cover and refrigerate at least 2 hours or up to 5 days. Makes about 1⅓ cups (315 ml).

2. To make the salad: Position a rack in the center of the oven and preheat the oven to 350°F (180°C). Spread the pecans on a small rimmed baking sheet (quarter-sheet pan) and bake, stirring occasionally, until toasted, about 10 minutes. Let cool completely. Coarsely chop the pecans and set aside.

3. Cook the bacon in a large skillet over medium heat, turning occasionally, until crisp and nicely browned, 8 to 10 minutes. Transfer to paper towels to drain and cool. Coarsely chop the bacon and set aside.

4. Using a food processor fitted with the thinnest slicing blade, a mandoline, a plastic V-slicer, or a large knife, cut the Brussels sprouts into very thin shreds. (If your cutter has a guard—use it! The round sprouts like to roll around.) Transfer to a large bowl. Add the dressing and toss well. Spread on a serving platter, sprinkle with the pecans, bacon, and blue cheese, and serve.

KALE AND DRIED CHERRY SALAD WITH SHERRY-THYME VINAIGRETTE

MAKES 4 TO 6 SERVINGS

Kale salads are ubiquitous these days, but they are not all created equal. At EMILY, we prefer to use purple baby kale, which is much more tender and sweeter than the typical varieties. With all kale salad, however, the trick is to massage the leaves with salt to break up the fibers—this is helpful even with the baby kale. Once this is done, add the dressing and toss.

SHERRY-THYME VINAIGRETTE

¼ cup (60 ml) sherry vinegar

1½ tablespoons fresh lemon juice

2 tablespoons coarsely chopped fresh thyme

½ teaspoon Dijon mustard

½ teaspoon stone-ground mustard

Kosher salt

½ cup (120 ml) canola or rice bran oil

¼ cup (25 g) coarsely chopped red onion

SALAD

8 ounces (225 g) baby kale (preferably purple, about 8 loosely packed cups)

½ teaspoon kosher salt

½ cup (120 g) Sherry-Thyme Vinaigrette (above), as needed

3 tablespoons dried tart cherries

3 tablespoons freshly grated pecorino Romano

1. To make the vinaigrette: Process the sherry vinegar, lemon juice, thyme, mustards, and ½ teaspoon salt in a blender until the thyme is finely minced. With the machine running, gradually pour the oil through the opening in the lid to make a thick vinaigrette. Turn off the machine, add the red onion, and pulse until the onion is minced. Season to taste with additional salt. Transfer to a lidded container. Cover and refrigerate for up to 3 days. Shake well before serving.

2. To make the salad: Put the kale in a large bowl and sprinkle with the salt. Rub the kale between your fingertips to incorporate the salt and tenderize the leaves.

3. Add the vinaigrette and cherries and toss. Divide the salad among four to six dinner plates. Sprinkle with the Romano and serve immediately.

SPINACH, CUCUMBER, AND MINT SALAD WITH PISTACHIO DRESSING

MAKES 4 SERVINGS

With its radicchio (we use the Treviso variety whenever we can find it) and dark green spinach and mint leaves, this salad pops with color. Ribbons of cucumber shavings and a sprinkle of peanuts finish off this very light and refined salad. The buttery flavor of pistachio oil mellows the vinaigrette.

PISTACHIO DRESSING
1½ tablespoons bottled yuzu juice or fresh lime juice
1½ tablespoons fresh lemon juice
⅓ cup (75 ml) plus 1 tablespoon extra-virgin olive oil
2 tablespoons pistachio oil
Kosher salt

SALAD
8 ounces (225 g) baby spinach
2 Persian cucumbers, cut into thin ribbons on a mandoline or V-slicer
6 radicchio leaves, preferably radicchio di Treviso, torn in half crosswise
    (if using round radicchio, tear the leaves into bite-sized pieces)
30 fresh mint leaves
½ cup (120 ml) Pistachio Dressing (above)
3 tablespoons coarsely chopped peanuts
Freshly ground black pepper

1. To make the dressing: Whisk the yuzu juice and lemon juice in a small bowl. Gradually whisk in the olive oil, followed by the pistachio oil. Season to taste with salt.

2. To make the salad: Toss the spinach, cucumbers, radicchio, and mint in a large bowl. Add the dressing and toss again. (Cover the remaining dressing and refrigerate for another use, up to 3 days.)

3. Divide the salad among four dinner plates. Sprinkle with the peanuts, season with the pepper, and serve immediately.

HEIRLOOM TOMATO AND WATERMELON SALAD

MAKE 4 TO 6 SERVINGS

This seasonal salad features two of summer's best ingredients. The watermelon pairs well with the olive oil and balsamic vinegar. We use white (sometimes called golden) balsamic to dress the salad, as traditional balsamic is dark.

> 2 tablespoons pitted and chopped kalamata olives
> 5 tablespoons (75 ml) extra-virgin olive oil
> 2 tablespoons white balsamic vinegar
> 1¼ pounds (570 g) cubed (1 inch/2.5 cm) seedless watermelon
> 2 heirloom tomatoes, seeded and cut into 1-inch (2.5-cm) cubes
> 1 tablespoon freshly grated pecorino Romano
> Freshly ground black pepper
> 4 to 6 fresh basil leaves

1. Purée the olives and 3 tablespoons of the oil in a blender. Transfer to a small bowl.

2. Whisk the white balsamic vinegar and remaining 2 tablespoons oil in a large bowl. Add the watermelon and tomatoes and toss gently.

3. Divide the mixture among four to six dinner plates. Drizzle each with the olive purée, sprinkle with the Romano, and finish with a grind of pepper. Add a basil leaf to each salad and serve immediately.

CHAPTER 3

PIZZA TOOLS AND INGREDIENTS

Matt identifies the pizza at EMILY as "fiercely American." While the lineage of pizza begins in Italy, it has been enhanced by chefs in America. Accordingly, we source our flour from American mills like King Arthur in Vermont and Central Milling in Utah, get our tomatoes from farmers in New Jersey, and look for local cheeses for our toppings. Our pizza is an amalgam of the best qualities from an array of pizza styles we know and love and eat way too much of. We are most inspired by New York, Connecticut, and Neapolitan styles of pizza. We stretch our dough thinly because we like a well-done thin crust with toppings spread evenly and generously across the dough, and while the crust is important, a pizza with too much exposed, naked crust that skimps on the sauce, cheese, and toppings is not an ideal pie. It's all about balance. Keep in mind that a too-heavy hand with toppings will lead to less than perfect pies. Though you see Matt tossing the dough here, we are just having fun. Our pies are rarely airborne.

THE PIZZA MAKER'S TOOLS

A pizza maker uses many tools that are fairly common and likely even found in a home kitchen, but there are a couple of essential additions. We start with two of the most important items you will need to make great pizza—an oven and a baking steel—and then move on to the tools in the order that you are most likely to use them.

Ovens

We have three ovens at our combined EMILY locations. Each oven has quirks (such as hot spots) that the baker learns to embrace or correct as needed. At our Clinton Hill location, our imported Pavesi oven, installed by Forza Forni, which we crowd-sourced in order to fund, is our pride and joy, and creates a 900ºF (482ºC) wood-fueled environment for round pizzas. In the West Village, we bake our round pizzas in a stately historic brick oven that dates back to the late 1800s and is one of the oldest working ovens in NYC. It is a gigantic oven that is 18 feet (5.5 m) deep, and it cranks up to a similar temperature as our oven in Brooklyn. For Detroit pies, we have a convection oven with a conveyor belt that perfectly times each pie as it moves from one end of the oven to the other. A fan blows the hot air (500ºF/260ºC) around the pan, which helps to evenly cook the pizza.

At home, short of building a wood-fired oven in your backyard, you will not be able to reach temperatures much above 550ºF (290ºC). Nonetheless, we have made slight adjustments in our recipes and techniques to be sure you'll still get incredible pizzas.

To sum up, pizza ovens are built to generate high temperatures of 800ºF (427ºC) or more. They have low ceilings so heat can radiate down onto the pizza for the golden brown topping we all crave. Round pizzas are cooked on the floor of a wood-burning pizza oven, which is impractical in a home oven that must be versatile enough to cook all kinds of food, not just pizza.

After many years of baking in a home oven and comparing the results to those from our restaurant ovens, here are our recommendations for the best home-baked pizzas:

- To improve top browning, place the oven rack in the top third of the oven, which is closer to the ceiling's radiant heat.
- Use a baking steel (preferred) or stone to simulate the hot floor of a pizza oven; this will help to brown the underskirt (bottom) of the pizza.
- Preheat the oven thoroughly at its highest setting with the steel/stone in place for at least 45 minutes for the oven to reach its optimum temperature and for the cooking surface to thoroughly absorb the heat. Do not skimp on the time—a full hour is even better.
- If your broiler is in the oven, turn it on High during the last 5 minutes of pre-heating to add a heat blast to increase the interior temperature even more.

Be sure to turn the oven back down to its highest non-broiling temperature setting before the pizza goes into the oven.

- If your baked pizza looks a little pale, turn on the broiler during the last minute or so to increase the final browning as desired. Be sure to keep a careful eye on it to avoid burning.

Baking steel

The original Baking Steel was created and trademarked by Andris Lagsdin, and we are his biggest fans. For years, the go-to baking surface was the *baking stone,* a porous ceramic rectangle. It worked okay, but over time it would inevitably chip, break, or get stained. A baking steel is much sturdier and altogether better. Made of a thick metal plate, it is extremely conductive and holds the oven heat so the pizza bottom bakes immediately on contact, with very little waiting for the heat to transfer. In side-by-side testing, we found the baking stone to bake a slightly drier crust. Our conjecture is that its porosity sucked some of the moisture from the dough.

A baking steel is the single best investment you can make to improve your pizza baking at home. You can use a baking stone, but if you are a truly serious budding pizza baker, you will want to upgrade to the steel.

Follow the manufacturer's instructions for seasoning the steel for its initial use, and for cleaning. Basically, treat the steel like cast iron and do not wash it with soap, which will remove the built-up seasoning and cause rusting.

Remember to always put the steel in the oven before preheating so it has plenty of time to reach the proper temperature. The minimum amount of time is 45 minutes, but an hour is even better.

Standing heavy-duty mixer

Our basic recipe requires a standing heavy-duty mixer with a dough hook for mixing and kneading, such as KitchenAid or Cuisinart. If you don't have this kind of mixer, it's another purchase that will totally up your cooking game.

We have also developed a mixer-free version of the dough for kitchens without mixers. However, the kneading does create a slightly more aerated dough with a looser crumb (meaning it has more visible air bubbles). For more on mixing the dough, see pages 60–66.

Digital scale

When it comes to measuring ingredients, we prefer to rely on the accuracy of metrics and weighing, rather than volume measure. There are simply too many variables when you measure flour by the cup. Due to its powdery texture and how it packs in the cup, the weight can be anywhere from 4 to 5 ounces (115 to 140 g). For most other ingredients, weighing is not as crucial. We use the metric system simply because it is much more precise than the bulky American system. When purchasing a scale, look for one that ranges from at least ½ ounce (1 g) to 11 pounds (5 kg).

If you are still a holdout, it is important to know that our measurement for flour is 130 grams of flour per cup, measured by the dip-and-sweep method. For more on this, see "An Important Note on Measuring" on page 46.

Bowl scraper

This flexible plastic tool has a rounded side that will scrape every last bit of dough out of the bowl.

Bench scraper

A sturdy rectangular metal blade with a handle on top, this is used to scrape and clean the work surface (called a bench by professional bakers) of leftover dough. Get in the habit of continually scraping your work area clean, or you will end up with dried clumps of dough in the crust. The bench scraper will also cut dough into portions so you don't have to go looking for a knife to do the job.

Wide plastic wrap

This may seem unnecessary to mention, but when you are covering relatively large amounts of dough, it is really helpful to have wide-width plastic wrap. The supermarket large roll is workable, but the super-wide (18-inch/46-cm) roll, sold at wholesale clubs and restaurant suppliers, is the way to go for covering large rimmed baking sheets (half-sheet pans) and big bowls.

Rubber bands

These come in very handy when you need to hold plastic film in place over balls of round pie dough during fermentation. If exposed to air, the surface will develop a tough film, and your dough will be ruined.

Plastic food containers

For bulk fermentation of the Detroit pie dough, you can simply refrigerate the dough in a mixing bowl. But the average bowl will take up a fair amount of unused space in the refrigerator. A round plastic food storage container with a cover, sold online and at restaurant suppliers, is very space-efficient, and airtight, too. A 2- to 3-quart (2- to 2.8-L) size is perfect.

Pizza peel

Made from wood or metal, this tool has a wide paddle on one end, with an attached handle. We prefer the metal peel for ease of use because its thin construction makes it easier to slip under a round of dough when necessary. Be sure your peel is at least 12 by 14 inches (30.5 by 35.5 cm) and has a moderately short handle.

Cutting board

Transfer a round or Detroit pie to a cutting board to cut it into slices or pieces. Never cut a pizza on a wooden pizza peel, as the sharp blade will cut right into the soft wood.

Wide spatula

A wide metal spatula is a useful helper for lifting a Detroit pie from its pan onto the cutting board. A wide bench scraper, also known as a bench knife, will work, too.

Pizza cutter

The rotating blade of a pizza cutter does quick work of slicing up a pizza. Our mantra when training new employees is "cut with confidence." We suggest a simple down and through, direct motion away from the body for ease of pizza cutting.

Pizza screens, pans, and racks

When pizza sits on a traditional aluminum pan, the bottom gives off trapped steam that eventually moistens the crust to make it soggy. A metal-mesh pizza screen lifts the pizza above the serving pan. Screens are quite inexpensive and will take your home-baked pizza up a few notches. For the round pies in this book, use 12-inch-diameter (30.5-cm) pizza pans and screens. There is no need to get fancy here, and aluminum pans and screens work well.

Baked Detroit pies are removed from their baking pans and transferred to 9 x 13-inch (23 x 33-cm) wire racks set in pans of the same size for serving. These small rimmed baking sheets are also called quarter-sheet pans, as they are a smaller version of the indispensible regular-sized rimmed baking sheets, or half-sheet pans, used as a workhorse in every professional kitchen.

You will find both the round and rectangular versions of the pans and their corresponding screens and racks at restaurant and pizzeria suppliers and online.

Plastic squeeze bottles

We like to apply finishes of honey, Sichuan oil, ranch dressing, and other condiments on some of our pizzas just before serving. Sure, you can drizzle any of these extras from a spoon, but applying them with a squeeze bottle lends ease and accuracy. Be sure you purchase food-grade bottles from a restaurant supplier.

PIZZA DOUGH INGREDIENTS

Dough, of course, is the backbone of any pizza. As raw dough ferments, it develops flavor as well as a strong internal structure that gives the crust its chewiness. Some pizza dough can be made quickly in an hour or so, but "fast" dough does not make world-class pizza. The only way to reach pizza nirvana is to let time do its job fermenting the dough for at least twenty-four hours to give it the desired flavor and texture, so be sure to think ahead.

We are known for two kinds of pizza: hand-shaped round pies baked on the floor of a wood-fired pizza oven, and thicker, rectangular Detroit pies with the dough baked directly in the baking pans. The basic ingredients for both are flour, water, yeast, and salt, with a little oil and sugar added to the Detroit pie dough. Each ingredient plays a very specific role. As each kind of dough is shaped for rising in a particular manner, the end results are entirely different. Directions for how to shape round and Detroit pies are detailed in separate chapters that follow.

The dough for the round pie is fermented under refrigeration in individual balls. However, the Detroit pie dough is fermented in bulk and then pressed into the pans for a final proofing (rising) at room temperature.

Because we make hundreds of pounds of dough a day at our restaurants, we are familiar with mixing the ingredients by machine. While that is our preferred method, it isn't the only one. We also have a no-knead dough that works well, too. The recipes for our round pie dough start on page 68. You'll find the Detroit pie dough recipes beginning on page 104.

In both the round and Detroit pie dough recipes, there's a crucial "ingredient" that is not listed: time. This element gives our dough the flavor that keeps the lines forming in front of our restaurants. The dough is fermented in the refrigerator for at least 24 hours before baking. This time period may seem lengthy, but in our opinion, a shorter time makes inferior pizza. So, think ahead! There's a two-day window for using the dough, or you can freeze and thaw it at your convenience.

Each dough recipe makes three pizzas. The round ones will be about 12 inches (30.5 cm) in diameter and yield 6 slices. The Detroit pies will measure about 11 x 7 inches (28 x 17 cm). We've developed recipes that allow you to either make three pizzas for a group of four to six, or to make one pizza serving two people. You can refrigerate (or freeze) two of the balls of dough for another meal.

Flour

Our favorite consumer flour of choice at EMILY is King Arthur bread flour, whose headquarters are in Vermont. It is an excellent product and well distributed throughout the country. We also like Central Milling in Utah, but their flour is mostly for professional bakers and not easy to find in stores.

Domestic flour for pizza requires a high protein content of at least 11.5 percent to create chewy, crisp dough with good structure. King Arthur comes in at an average of 12.7 percent, a full percentage point above most other brands. Two elements in wheat, gliadin and glutenin, combine with the protein gluten when moistened with water. Gluten is the invisible structure in dough that makes it stretch when carbon dioxide is released from the yeast during baking. Therefore, high-protein flours give the best results.

If you use other brands of bread flour, expect the baked crust to be slightly less chewy. The protein content of some flours is not listed on the packaging, but with online research or by contacting the producer, you can determine the exact number of your brand.

For round pie dough, we include rye flour. Rye has very low gluten content, so it reduces the gluten content in the dough while adding some flavor. Rye also has more natural sugar than wheat, and this has a positive affect on fermentation, giving the yeast more "food" to create the carbon-dioxide bubbles needed for good dough structure.

Water

You may notice that, unlike other many other recipes for pizza dough, we call for only a small amount of warm water to help dissolve the yeast. The specific temperature of 105º to 115ºF (40º to 45ºC) is needed to melt the coating on the tiny yeast granules. The water should simply feel like warm bath water, a little higher than body temperature. Never go above 138ºF (59ºC), which will kill any yeast, dry or fresh. After the active dry yeast is dissolved in warm water, it is mixed with cold water. The cooler water allows fermentation to progress at a slower pace, and the passage of time dramatically improves the flavor and texture of the dough. Unlike many typical dough recipes ours doesn't require the typical "warm, draft-free spot" to proof (raise) the dough. That would make the dough rise too quickly, and give inferior results.

The amount of water is crucial to successful pizza dough. Gluten is not formed in dough until the flour is moistened. A moist dough will be more elastic and allow more gas bubbles to form. The percentage of water to flour indicates the dough's hydration level. Our dough comes in at about 68 percent hydration; any dough over 65 percent is considered high hydration. This means the dough is a bit too wet to mix by hand in standard kneading on a work surface. We provide two methods, one in a standing heavy-duty mixer (such as KitchenAid) as well as a low-tech, no-knead version that doesn't use a mixer.

In a nutshell, no-knead dough works because as the dough sits, the water works with the gluten to form the dough structure. Traditionally, dough is kneaded because the action strengthens the gluten matrix. At the restaurant, we find it easier to knead big batches in the mixer, and we still do it at home out of habit. Both methods make equally excellent dough, so do not stress over the choice.

One final, and huge, piece of advice: When making dough, *weigh your water*! Because of the nature of liquid measuring cups, where liquid is added to correspond with a mark on the side of the vessel, it's very easy to measure an imprecise amount of water. With dough, where the proportion of flour and water is critical, a couple of tablespoons can make a big difference.

Yeast

Most pizza masters prefer fresh (also called cake or compressed) yeast because it is easy to dissolve and revives itself from its hibernating state more quickly than dehydrated active dry yeast. The main issue with fresh yeast is that it's made for the consumer market only during the Easter and winter holiday baking seasons. True, it can be purchased in 1-pound (455 g) blocks at a restaurant supplier, but that's an awful lot to use before its expiration date, especially because our recipes use a very small amount of yeast for each batch. Finally, fresh yeast has a short shelf life, and to store it longer than a few days, it must be frozen, where it will keep for only three months or so.

That being said, active dry yeast is a very solid choice for pizza dough. It is commonly sold in ¼-ounce (7-gram) packets holding about 2¼ teaspoons each. It is also available in 4-ounce (113-g) glass jars or sold in even larger amounts in bulk. In any case, store the yeast in a jar or another kind of airtight container (especially after you open a packet) in the refrigerator and use it by the expiration date. Yeast loses its power as it ages, so it's a good idea not to buy too much ahead of time.

Instant (also called rapid-rise or bread-machine) yeast is yet another type of yeast. Its advantage is that it is easy to find (in fact, it's surpassing active dry in popularity and availability at supermarkets) and it doesn't need a specific water temperature for mixing—cold water works just fine, or you can use warm water.

You may be surprised at the small amount of yeast in our dough. Some recipes for round pie dough call for a full packet of yeast to raise the dough in the minimum time before forming and baking. We use a small amount of commercial yeast to attract the natural wild yeasts in the environment, which combine with the commercial yeast to make a better-tasting dough. The Detroit pie, which should be somewhat puffy with lots of air bubbles, has more yeast (but still much less than usually called for) to ensure that enough carbon dioxide is created for that desired texture.

Allowing for personal taste and availability, we give measurements for both active dry and instant yeast. If you have fresh yeast, use the same amount as instant, but keep in mind that it may take some experimentation, allowing for the variances among brands of cake yeast. Also, it dissolves best in lukewarm (about 100°F/38°C) water.

Salt

In most table salt, additives are used to keep the salt from clumping, and they affect the flavor. Kosher salt, in addition to its flakiness, which can usually be detected on the tongue during eating for a textural dimension, is a much more natural product with better flavor, and many chefs (including our team at EMILY) won't use any other kind.

The most important distinction is not just flavor, but the difference between the size and shape of the crystals among the types and even brands. Because of these variables, a teaspoon of table salt does not weigh the same as the same amount of kosher salt. Even more surprising, within the kosher category, the two most common brands, Diamond Crystal and Morton, are much different by volume.

We prefer Diamond Crystal kosher salt, which comes in red-and-white containers. The 3-pound (1.4-kg) box is ubiquitous in East Coast supermarkets, although it is also sold in a 13-ounce (370-g) canister. It has a very clean flavor, and the salt crystals are actually flakes. However, on the West Coast, Morton (packed in similar sizes) is the most common brand, with visibly larger crystals than Diamond Crystal. It's important to note that these crystals are hollow, so they measure much differently.

If you use a different brand than Diamond Crystal kosher salt, you must adjust the amount when measuring by volume. To use Morton kosher salt, decrease the amount by a scant half. (For example, in our recipes, 1 teaspoon becomes a rounded ½ teaspoon.) These changes are especially important with the dough recipes. For that reason, we give the salt's weight.

The amount of salt is a very important element in the dough. Of course, it flavors the dough, and undersalted pizza crust tastes flat. But salt is also crucial to proofing, or raising the dough. (Fermentation raises the dough under refrigeration, and the rise occurs at a much slower pace for better flavor.) Without salt, the yeast will multiply at a pretty reckless rate, and the dough will overinflate before the flavor has a chance to develop. Extra salt will make the proofing slow down. There is a "just right" amount.

For a final seasoning of savory dishes, we use Maldon sea salt from British waters, identified by its large flakes. There is no advantage to using pricey Maldon salt in your pizza dough.

Sugar

Dough rises when the live yeast cells "eat" the natural carbohydrates in the flour, producing carbon dioxide as a waste product. This gas is trapped in the dough to make bubbles that inflate the dough. We add a bit of extra sugar to our pan dough, not so much as a sweetener, but as food to feed the yeast and ensure a softer baked crust with lots of air bubbles. It also improves the browning of the crust.

Oil

Not all pizza bakers put olive oil in their dough. We find it adds an odd flavor when the dough is baked in our hot ovens, but we do want some oil in the Detroit pie dough to make it easier to stretch. We like to use a relatively flavorless oil, such as canola or vegetable. These oils can withstand high temperatures, a feature that's useful when baking the Detroit pies in a very hot oven.

AN IMPORTANT NOTE ON MEASURING

Because there are so many good and inexpensive digital kitchen scales on the market, we made the decision to use only the metric system as an alternative to American volume measurements. These days, every digital scale can toggle between metric and American weights. If you ever want to increase or decrease a recipe yield, it's much easier to do so in metric instead of dealing with teaspoons and cups as well as the ounces and pounds of the volume system.

For this book, we are following standard cookbook style and offering metric weights only for ingredients above 3¾ tablespoons by volume. We have also rounded off to the nearest increment of 0 or 5, so you don't have to feel that you must measure precisely 123 grams of an ingredient for the recipe to work. There are those who will disagree, but 2 or 3 grams of anything (okay, maybe salt) just isn't going to ruin the dish. We do use precise measurements for the four pizza dough recipes.

Semisolid ingredients, such as mayonnaise and yogurt, are measured by cup and their milliliter equivalent. A little bit more or less of these foods isn't crucial. If you wish, you can measure them in volume measuring cups and level off the excess at the top.

As for the flour, we use the spoon-and-sweep method for measuring. This entails spooning the flour into a volume measuring cup and sweeping off the excess at the top rim of the cup with a knife or other flat utensil. (This is in opposition to the other method, known as dip-and-sweep, where the cup is dipped into the ingredient and then leveled. This method can yield 15 to 20 grams more flour per cup.) For our recipes, we figure 130 grams of flour per cup. You can use measuring spoons for smaller amounts of less than 3¾ tablespoons.

Once you start following a recipe in one system, do not toggle back and forth to the other, as in metric to volume or vice versa.

THE SAUCES

You've chosen whether to make round or Detroit pie, and the dough is fermenting in the fridge. Now, what kind of sauce are you in the mood for? On EMILY's menu, you'll see the pizzas grouped by color: red (tomato), white (no sauce, just cheese), pink (red sauce with vodka and cream), and a green (tomatillo) sauce.

Keep in mind that the "sauce" for some of the best pizzas in the world is just crushed canned tomatoes. That being said, we do use a simmered red sauce for our Detroit pies. Also, it is characteristic for some of the Detroit pies to be finished with stripes of sauce after the cheese and toppings have been added. Of course, traditional round pizza gets the familiar layering of sauce, cheese, and toppings.

RED SAUCE

MAKES ABOUT 2¼ CUPS (540 ML)

Our round pies are usually made with the classic topping of crushed tomatoes. For our Detroit pies, we like this modified marinara sauce. We prefer to simmer the seasoning ingredients in wine, then add crushed tomatoes at the end so they retain their bright flavor and color. Leftover sauce can be frozen and used for more pizzas or pasta.

> 3 tablespoons Garlic Oil (page 207)
> ⅔ cup (65 g) finely chopped yellow onion
> 6 cloves Garlic Confit (page 207), chopped
> ½ cup (120 ml) dry white wine
> One 28-ounce (784-g) can crushed tomatoes
> 1 teaspoon dried oregano
> Kosher salt

1. Heat the garlic oil in a medium saucepan over medium heat. Add the onion and cook, stirring occasionally, until it is translucent but not browned, about 3 minutes. Stir in the garlic confit and pour in the wine. Increase the heat to high and boil until the wine is reduced by half, 3 to 5 minutes.

2. Remove from the heat and let cool completely. Purée the mixture in a blender. Add the tomatoes and oregano and pulse just to combine. Season to taste with salt. (The sauce can be covered and refrigerated for up to 3 days or frozen for up to 2 months.)

Crushed tomatoes Many people insist on using San Marzano plum tomatoes for pizza and other Italian fare. San Marzanos are excellent, but they aren't the only great tomato in the world. New Jersey, known as the Garden State, has long been famous for its produce, and its tomatoes are renowned. We exclusively use crushed tomatoes from Jersey Fresh, a farming cooperative that produces different local brands. They have a very bright flavor with a good tart-sweet balance, a gorgeous red color, and a moderately coarse texture that can be easily spread over dough. California also grows some amazing tomatoes, so look for crushed tomatoes from the Golden State in West Coast markets.

Experiment with various brands to find a favorite. Some are too chunky (more chopped than crushed), and others are too puréed and saucy. Regardless of what brand you prefer for flavor, you may still need to process the tomatoes in a blender to a slightly coarse purée. This "raw" puree will be cooked under high heat in the oven, so in our opinion, there is really no need to simmer it first with seasonings.

VODKA SAUCE

Alcohol has the ability to pump up the flavors of other ingredients, and vodka proves this is so in this recipe. Leftover sauce? We probably don't have to tell you to serve it with pasta!

1 tablespoon unsalted butter
½ cup (75 g) finely chopped red onion
½ teaspoon hot red pepper flakes
3 tablespoons vodka
One 28-ounce (784-g) can crushed tomatoes
3 tablespoons soy sauce
⅔ cup (165 ml) heavy cream

1. Melt the butter in a medium saucepan over medium heat. Add the red onion and cover. Cook, stirring occasionally, until the onion is tender and translucent but not browned, about 5 minutes. Stir in the hot red pepper flakes.

2. Add the vodka, allowing the heat of the saucepan to create a burst of steam and cook off the alcohol. Stir in the tomatoes and soy sauce and bring to a boil over high heat. Reduce the heat to medium-low and cook at a steady simmer until slightly reduced, 10 to 15 minutes. During the last 5 minutes, stir in the cream. Remove from the heat and let cool completely.

3. Using a hand blender, purée the sauce in the saucepan. (Or, in batches, purée it in a blender.) Transfer the sauce to a lidded container, cover, and refrigerate for up to 3 days.

TOMATILLO SAUCE

MAKES ABOUT 3 CUPS (720 ML)

This verdant salsa verde is the one we use for our green pizzas. Made with tomatillos, jalapeños, and cilantro, we are inspired to bring Mexican flavor profiles into our kitchen. Not all versions of this green sauce broil the chiles and garlic cloves, but we think that's the key to making the best version. Leftovers are excellent served as a dip with tortilla chips or raw vegetables.

> 2 large, fresh jalapeños
> 6 garlic cloves, peeled (do not crush while peeling)
> 1 pound (455 g) tomatillos, husked, rinsed, and patted dry
> 1 small yellow onion, chopped
> 1 cup (50 g) packed fresh cilantro leaves and tender stems
> 1 teaspoon sugar
> 1 teaspoon kosher salt

1. Position a broiler rack about 6 inches (15 cm) from the heat source and preheat the broiler to High. Put the jalapeños and garlic in the broiler pan. Broil, turning them as needed, until the garlic is browned, 5 to 7 minutes. Transfer the garlic to a plate and continue broiling the jalapeños until the skins are blackened and blistered, being careful not to burn through to the flesh, 2 to 3 minutes more. Transfer the jalapeños to the plate. Let stand for a few minutes. When the jalapeños are cool enough, rub off and discard the blackened skin. Cut the jalapeños open and discard the seeds.

2. In two or three batches, purée the tomatillos, peeled jalapeños, browned garlic, onion, cilantro, sugar, and salt in a blender. Do not add any water. The sauce must be very smooth, as in some recipes it will be squeezed through a plastic bottle. Transfer to a lidded container, cover, and refrigerate for up to 3 days or freeze for up to 2 months. If the thawed sauce separates, process in a blender before serving.

THE CHEESES

Cheese that is destined to be a pizza topping is usually judged by its ability to melt easily, although flavor certainly comes into play. Too often, a pizza is all about the cheese. With our pizzas, the emphasis is on how the ingredients come together to make a superior eating experience. Try using less cheese than your intuition might suggest so all the components of the pies can shine.

Mozzarella and Burrata

One of the distinctions we make between our thin-crust round pie and the thicker Detroit pie is the kind of mozzarella used for the topping. The round pies call for *artisan-style fresh mozzarella*. For our Detroit pie, we use a *low-moisture mozzarella* that can be found in the grocery store.

If we lived in southern Italy, we would insist on *mozzarella di bufula*, made from water buffalo milk, for our pizza. But we don't, and we're very fond of cow's milk mozzarella. We make ours in-house with curd purchased from a cheesemonger. *Mozza* means "cut" in Italian, and it describes how the warm curd is cut up in a pot. The curds are then kneaded and stretched in very hot water until they can be shaped into a ball. Working the curds in hot water shows the dedication of the cheese maker because the water must be painfully hot to keep the cheese from cooling and setting up.

If you are not planning to make your mozzarella from scratch, many large-scale cheese makers sell "fresh" mozzarella. These whole-milk mozzarella balls are often sold packed in individual whey-filled tubs, or each handmade ball is wrapped in plastic. It is highly perishable, so only buy what you will eat in a few days.

Unlike low-moisture mozzarella, which can be purchased already shredded or sliced, fresh mozzarella is sliced at home into rounds about ¼-inch (6-mm) thick. As you slice from the outside of the ball to the inside, the size of the rounds will change. If the rounds seem too large (say, more than 3 inches/7.5 cm in diameter), just tear them in half. If the slices are too big or thick, they will not melt evenly. Use your thinnest knife for cutting the cheese. A wire cheese cutter works even better.

When it comes to low-moisture mozzarella, we prefer the whole-milk kind to the part-skim for its richer flavor. Buy your mozzarella in blocks, not already shredded, because the shredded variety is sometimes coated with superfluous anti-caking ingredients. Shred the chilled direct-from-the-fridge mozzarella on the large holes of a box shredder, or use a food processor.

If the mozzarella seems too warm to shred easily, pop it in the freezer for 30 minutes or so to firm it up. Whole-block mozzarella, wrapped in plastic, can be refrigerated for at least two weeks, but once shredded (and stored in a zip-tight plastic bag) it will last for only a week or so.

Burrata, which can be found in cheese stores and specialty markets, is a variation on fresh mozzarella, with a creamy interior wrapped in a mozzarella shell, and is always sold packed in water. Because of its delicate texture, it's not baked on the crust. Instead, we add it to finished pizza just before serving and let the radiating heat warm it through.

Cheddar

We use a few different kinds of Cheddar at EMILY, all with specific purposes.

Mild Cheddar, combined with low-moisture mozzarella, gives our Detroit pie its distinctive *frico,* or crisp, golden brown perimeter. You can use either the yellow or white kind, but it's best to buy block cheese and shred it at home to avoid unwanted additives. *Cheddar curds,* another favorite cheese from the Midwest, is used on The Camp Randall pizza (page 74). These are simply curds of sharp Cheddar that have not been pressed into a block.

Sharp Cheddar, from Grafton Village in Vermont, is a crucial ingredient of our EMMY Burger. While any small-batch, high-quality Cheddar will do, we are huge fans of Grafton and recommend it without reservation.

Havarti

Though originally made in Denmark, there are many good domestic versions of this creamy, semi-soft cheese. It melts very well and is a good addition to your list of eligible cheeses for pizza.

Pecorino Romano

Two aged grating cheeses are beloved ingredients in Italian cuisine: *Parmigiano-Reggiano* and *pecorino Romano.* (And to a minor extent, aged Asiago.) They are far from interchangeable. We prefer Romano because its bold (some might say funky) flavor stands up well to other assertive pizza toppings like spicy pepperoni and tart tomatoes. Also, it is the authentic, preferred cheese for Neapolitan-style pizza.

We use so much pecorino Romano at EMILY we gave it a nickname: pec. However, there are at least three Italian sheep's milk cheeses named pecorino sold in the States. Pay attention to the second half of the name, which corresponds with where the cheese is made. A well-stocked cheese store may sell pecorino Toscano (from Tuscany) or a pecorino Sardo (from Sardinia), but they will always carry pecorino Romano, made in Lazio, the area around Rome. Some Toscano and Sardo pecorinos are sold in their young, semihard states to eat as a table cheese, but Romano is aged until it's hard enough to grate and use as a cooking ingredient. Pecorino is a cheese of southern Italy, as traditionally there is more land suitable for grazing sheep than pasturing cows.

Always buy imported Italian Romano cheese. The standard bearer for Romano is the Locatelli brand. It should be freshly grated by hand on the small holes on a grater. Although Locatelli is often sold pre-grated, we buy ours in a block and grate it ourselves. A wedge of Romano, well wrapped and refrigerated, will keep for at least a month, but the grated version may start to mold after a couple of weeks.

Ricotta

Moist and creamy *ricotta* makes a great topping, but it works best in combination with other cheeses to balance its wetness and mild flavor. Because it's so simple (and fun) to make by hand, we skip the commercial version and make our own (see the recipe on page 208).

Ricotta means "recooked" in Italian because, in the traditional method, it is made from the leftover whey produced by other cheeses. For a richer ricotta, we use whole milk for our in-house ricotta. It is sometimes available at cheese stores and Italian delicatessens. Fresh ricotta, which does not have any preservatives, is very perishable, and lasts only a few days refrigerated. Always stir fresh ricotta well before using it to incorporate any whey that may have separated out.

In a pinch, you can substitute commercial whole-milk ricotta sold at supermarkets in plastic tubs. To improve and enrich it, stir 1 to 2 tablespoons heavy cream into each ½ cup (120 g).

THE TOPPINGS

Our approach to topping combinations is simple: we play, we experiment, and we apply toppings that we like. We hope that you'll enjoy some of our classic combos but we encourage you to create your own personal topping mixtures. All parts of the pizza are equally important. Avoid the temptation to overload your pizza. We source the best ingredients for our pie toppings. We are dedicated to using local producers for our American pizza, and are not locked into imported foods just because they are traditional. Our cured meats come from nearby purveyors who have become masters in their field. We actually prefer Jersey tomatoes to Italian. We dry fresh oregano instead of insisting on the Sicilian variety.

Meats

We have a wide selection of plant-based pizza toppings, but our guests love traditional meat toppings, too. *Pepperoni,* that narrow cured sausage that seems to exist solely as a pizza topping (you rarely hear of anyone having a pepperoni sandwich, right?) is in every supermarket. Too often, it's loaded with chemicals to keep it shelf-stable. Look for an Italian salami producer near you that also makes great pepperoni and have it freshly sliced.

Bacon, Italian sausage, chorizo (the soft Mexican kind, not hard Spanish links), and *ground beef* all make appearances on our pizzas. In all cases, we parcook the meats in a skillet just until they lose their raw look, as they will cook more and brown in the oven. If you use raw meat products as toppings, they may render fat and juices on the pizza and make it soggy. Specific directions are given in each recipe for how to prepare each meat.

Vegetables

Red onion and *green bell pepper* are used as flavor elements in some of our toppings. To be sure that they don't weigh down the crust, we cut them into thin half-moon-shaped strips. If the vegetables are thick or chunky, they are simply too heavy for our thin dough. We prefer red onions to yellow (Spanish) ones and green bell peppers to red ones because they have sharper flavors that work well in our topping combinations.

The procedure is similar for both peppers and onions. Lay the vegetable on its side and cut off the top and bottom in ½-inch (12-mm) slices. Set these aside to slice later or save for another use. Cut the vegetable of choice in half lengthwise. For the bell pepper, trim out and discard the ribs and seeds. Place the vegetable on its flat cut side and cut into thin half-moon-shaped slices about ⅛ inch (3 mm) thick. For the onions, separate the rings into individual strips.

Castelvetrano Olives

We only truly like a single kind of olive, the Castelvetrano variety. We find other kinds too sour, bitter, or hard. The Sicilian Castelvetrano variety is a true olive green color, and cured with salt and food-safe lye to give the olives an especially tender texture, making them easy to pit.

Pitted Castelvetrano olives are not as common as kalamatas, so you will probably have to pit them yourself. Skip the olive pitter—there is a much easier, gadget-free way. Place a few olives at a time under the wide, flat side of a large chef's knife on a work surface. Using the heel of your hand, rap on the blade to smash the olives. Pick out the loosened pits, and you're done. Most of the time, the olives have split into halves, but if not, just tear them apart.

Pickled Peppers

We have a fondness for sharp and spicy pickled peppers, which do a lot to enliven any pizza. We use three kinds: hot cherry peppers, banana peppers, and jalapeños. We also like the zing from the pickling juices combined with the peppery heat.

The first two we purchase in jars. *Cherry peppers,* which are sold both red and green and mild or hot, are sold sliced, but you're more likely to find them whole. In the latter case, cut them into rounds about ¼ inch (6 mm) thick before using. Bright yellow *banana peppers* are usually sold sliced. We make our own *Pickled Jalapeños* (page 209), but in a pinch, the store-bought slices, used to top nachos, will work. In all cases, drain the peppers briefly on paper towels to remove excess moisture.

Home-Dried Oregano

We prefer dried oregano to fresh because drying oregano concentrates its natural oils to actually increase its flavor. Also, dried oregano is easier to crumble and distribute evenly on the pizza than fresh leaves.

But commercial dried oregano can look and smell fine but taste musty. To fix the problem, we began drying fresh bunches in our own kitchen. Now we have dried oregano that crumbles beautifully and has an irresistible distinct scent that says "pizza."

To dry your own oregano, start with a big bunch of fresh and sprightly sprigs. (The amount is immaterial, but don't make more than you will use up in a few weeks.) Separate the sprigs and spread them out in a single layer on a baking sheet. Position a rack in the center of the oven and preheat the oven to 200ºF (95ºC). Turn off the oven (this is important). Put the baking sheet in the oven and prop the oven door open with a wooden spoon. Dry the oregano in the turned-off oven until the leaves are crisp, about 20 minutes, though the oregano will be fine for up to an hour. Remove the leaves from the stems, discarding the stems and keeping the leaves as intact as possible. Store the oregano leaves in airtight wide-mouthed jars in a cool, dark place for up to two months. If you prefer to use bottled oregano, choose a high-quality imported Italian or Sicilian brand, preferably with the leaves still on the stems.

Regardless of the kind of dried oregano you use, there is a special way to sprinkle it. Using your first two fingers combined with your thumb, grab a large pinch of the leaves out of the jar. When sprinkling, crumble and crush the leaves to release their oil and aroma. This "pinch and crumble" action is much more effective than simple scattering the leaves.

Fresh Basil

At EMILY, we use only fresh basil on our pizzas and only put basil on pies once they have come out of the oven. In our experience, dried basil lacks the aroma and texture of fresh basil leaves, and cooked basil changes flavor and wilts in the heat. A bouquet of fresh basil evokes the smell of summer, and we feel lucky that the hydroponics movement is really taking force, because it allows us as well as home cooks like yourself the opportunity to procure bright, fresh basil in supermarkets year-round.

We will experiment with various kinds of basil as our purveyors offer them, but for everyday cooking, you can't go wrong with the standard garden-variety basil, Genoa (also called Italian, Genovese, and large leaf). Outside of the summer season, look for a good hydroponic option. Be mindful to not buy basil in large quantities, as it wilts and blackens easily in the fridge. The best way to store it is to place the bunch, like a bouquet, in a glass of water. Tent a plastic bag over the top and store either in or out of the fridge for two to three days.

When using basil as a garnish for pizza, we take a less is more approach. We scatter some fresh leaves over the top of the baked pizza and leave it at that. We don't chop the leaves at all. If the leaves are large, the guests can tear them into little pieces and sprinkle them over the pizza.

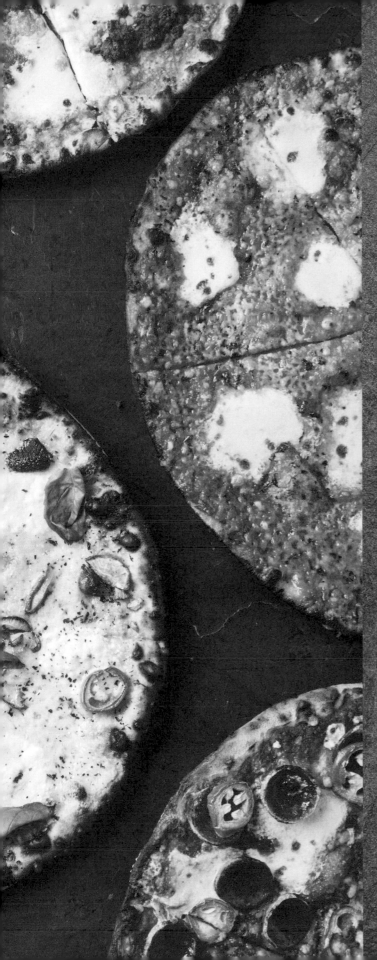

CHAPTER 4

ROUND PIES

Most people have memories of pizza from their childhood, and we love to evoke that sense of nostalgia for our guests. So, we are helping make new pizza memories with creatively topped pies as well as updated versions of old favorites.

Though we all share collective memories of pizza dough being tossed into the air, this is something you will not see often done at EMILY. We stretch on the counter because the method creates a more even disc and also less of a mess. We have worked hard to create dough that is flavorful and can stretch easily enough to be ready for the oven in a minute or so. It is much easier than you think to make a ball of dough and turn it into a thin, flat disc. If you are a novice pizza maker, remember that the craft is always a work in progress, and each time you stretch you are learning, building muscle memory, and getting a hands-on feel for how to work with dough. Above all, pizza making is fun, especially at home with friends or family, so enjoy the process!

MAKING OUR ROUND PIES

While a homemade pizza might feel like a challenge, there are surefire techniques, which are teachable and learnable. Pizza is a craft that takes time to master, so allow yourself the freedom to be present and have fun while making the pizza—know that every time you stretch and cook your pies, they will improve!

Make the Dough: Start with a fresh batch of Round Pie Dough made by the mixer (page 68) or no-knead (page 69) method. Either recipe will make three 12-inch (30.5-cm) pizzas.

Cut the Dough into Thirds: Using a bowl scraper, scrape the dough out of the bowl onto a lightly floured work surface. Weigh the dough; it should be about 900 grams. Divide the number by three to get the weight for each ball. Using the bench knife or a chef's knife, cut the dough into thirds.

Weigh the Dough: Weigh each portion on a kitchen scale, trimming and adding bits of dough from each portion as needed to get the right amount. Each portion should weigh about 300 grams. Remember that there will be a little dough left in the bowl and on the spoon, so the weights will vary by a few grams one way or the other. Don't stress out over this.

Round the Dough: Next, you'll round each portion into a smooth ball with a taut skin. This tight surface (called a cloak) is important because it creates equal surface tension so the ball rises evenly. Rounding works best on a barely floured work surface, as some traction is necessary.

Very lightly oil a glass or metal baking pan, 9 x 13 inches (23 x 33 cm), and set it nearby to hold the finished balls. In the restaurant, we use flour during this pro-

cess, but for home cooking, the oil will help keep the balls separate and less sticky, hence easier to use. Place one ball with its smoothest side up on the work surface. Lightly cup your hands and place them on the opposite sides of the ball. Using the bottoms of your cupped hands, tuck the sides of the ball under the mass, stretching the top of the dough a bit at the same time. Rotate the ball and repeat tucking and stretching the sides. Repeat this action a few times, and the ball will gradually shape itself and become smooth and taut. Pinch the folds on the bottom of the ball together. Transfer to the prepared pan. Repeat with the remaining balls.

Cover the Dough Balls: Cover the pan with plastic wrap. Hold the wrap in place with a couple of rubber bands—if the plastic comes off in the refrigerator during fermentation, the dough will dry out and be useless.

Ferment the Dough: Refrigerate the covered pan of dough for at least 24 or up to 48 hours. The dough will grow noticeably larger, but it will not necessarily double

Preheat the Oven: At least 45 minutes before baking, place the baking steel or stone in the upper third of the oven and preheat the oven to 525ºF (220ºC). You'll need this much time to thoroughly heat the steel or stone.

Bench-Rest the Dough: Remove the dough in its pan from the refrigerator. Let it stand, covered, at room temperature on the work surface for at least 30 or up to 45 minutes to lose its chill. As the dough warms up, it will become very stretchable. The dough should not be brought to room temperature but should warm enough that it becomes more pliable.

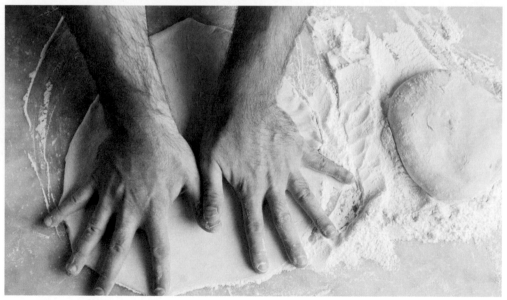

Pat the Dough into a Disc: Flour the work surface well. Transfer a dough ball to the work surface, keeping the other balls covered. Dust the top of the dough with flour. Using your palms, press and stretch the dough into a thick disc. From this point, use your fingertips to dimple and stretch the dough, working from the center out, to stretch it into a thinner disc about 7 inches (17.5 cm) across. If the dough snaps back, it may be too cold, so cover it and let it rest for about 5 minutes. Scrape any bits of clinging dough from the work surface with the bench knife.

Stretch the Dough: Making sure your hands are well floured, slip them, palms down, under the dough. Move both hands along the edge of the round, letting the

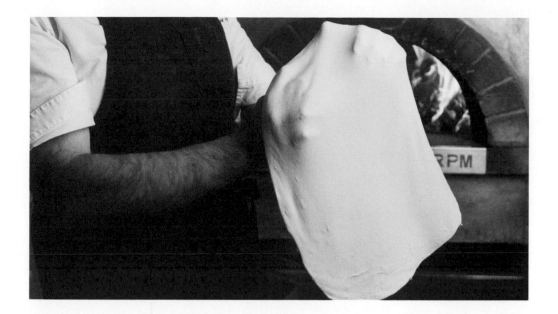

dough hang down and allowing gravity to pull it down as you stretch it. This is a little like moving your hands around the circumference of a steering wheel. As you work around the dough, move your hands apart slightly to stretch the edge of the dough even more. The dough in the center will take care of itself. Keep moving your hands around the outer edge of the dough until you have made about two full rotations. If the dough is warm enough, this will all happen surprisingly fast, and you could have a fully stretched round of pizza dough in 30 seconds.

Check the Size of the Dough: Lay the dough on the work surface and check the size. You are aiming for a 12-inch (30.5-cm) round. If you want to make the dough slightly larger, try this: Keeping the dough on the work surface, use both hands to pinch and stretch the dough as you move around the edges of the round.

Slide the Dough onto the Peel: Note that when you put the dough round on the peel is a personal choice based on the kind of peel you own. At the restaurants, we build each pizza on a marble counter, add the toppings immediately, and then slide a thin metal pizza peel under the round. Many home bakers own a thicker wooden peel, which is not ideal for sliding under a topped pizza. If you are using a wooden peel, it is better to build the pizza on the peel. Be sure the peel is nicely floured with a thin but fairly even layer of flour to keep the round from sticking. Place the peel next to the dough and quickly slide the dough onto the peel. Adjust the dough as needed on the peel so it's flat and as evenly round as possible.

If the pizza round is a bit too misshapen for your liking, here is a useful trick: Hook the top edge of the dough round (¼ inch/6 mm or so) over the top edge of the pizza peel to secure it. With the top edge stationed in place, it will be easier to stretch the remaining, lower part of the dough into the shape you want.

Don't get overly hung up on the size or shape of the pizza—it's completely okay for some pizzas to be a bit larger, a bit smaller, or a bit more ovular or even square-like. Not all delicious pizzas are perfectly round. Sometimes the pizza will change

shape when it comes off the peel into the oven, and when working in such an artisanal modality, it's natural for shape and size to come out uniquely.

Top the Dough: The dough is now ready for topping. We prefer a thin crust with toppings spread evenly and to the edges across the whole disc. And while crust is sacred, too much crust with not enough sauce, cheese, and toppings is not ideal in our opinion. Keep in mind: while it is tempting to overload the pizza with toppings, a heavy pizza will be difficult to slide onto the peel and will likely be soggy after baking.

Be sure that all of the topping components are ready to use—that the cheese is grated, the meat is parcooked, and any previously cooked ingredients are cooled.

For a red pizza, start with a thin layer of canned crushed tomatoes. We use a shallow 2-ounce (60-ml) food-service portion spoon with a red handle. These spoons have standardized colors that identify their size. This gives us the right amount of sauce every time. As another option, you can accomplish the same thing with a ¼-cup (60-ml) measuring cup. Use the underside of the scoop (or cup) to spread the sauce on the disc to make a border that is as thin as possible, which is about ¼ inch (6 mm) wide. We like a well-done thin crust, which is unlike the bigger, puffy crust of our Neopolitan predecessor.

When applying the rest of the toppings, take care to distribute them evenly. Each pie will be cut into six pieces, so be sure to scatter the toppings so that each slice includes some of each ingredient. You can just eyeball this. We encourage you to make sure the toppings don't concentrate in the middle of the pizza; instead, spread them evenly and make sure to place them all the way to the very edge of the dough, so the crust will be minimal and crunchy and you will have a maximum palette of topped pie.

Be sure to parcook meats (see page 55) before adding to pizza. If not cooked first, they will give off their juices and fat, making the crust soggy.

If you are using a thin metal pizza peel, slip it under the pizza. Readjust the dough as needed on the peel.

Bake the Pizza: The pizza should go in the oven as quickly as possible. Give the dough on the peel a couple of sharp horizontal shakes to be sure it is loose and sliding on the peel. If not, lift up the offending portion and toss a little flour under it.

Open the oven door and put the far edge of the peel at the back of the steel or stone. Using a sharp movement with a snap of the wrist, slide the pizza onto the preheated steel or stone. Set a kitchen timer and try not to peek in the oven too often, as this will lower the oven temperature.

If you are making more than one pizza, just leave the dough out, covered, on your work surface. During the last minute or so before the first pizza is done, make

the second pizza. With practice, you'll be surprised how quickly you can stretch the dough. It's best not to stretch the dough any longer than two minutes or so before topping, or it might stick to the work surface.

Serve the Pizza: When the pizza is ready, use the peel to transfer it to a cutting board. We have designed these pizzas to be cut into 6 slices; use a pizza cutter to do this. Never cut the pizza on a wooden peel, as the blade will cut into the wood. Remember the axiom "Cut with confidence! Down and through." You will find that you have more control over the blade if you draw it away from, instead of toward, your body.

To serve the pizza as we do at EMILY, put the pieces on a wire-mesh pizza screen placed on a round aluminum pizza pan. This keeps the pizza elevated above the pan—otherwise, steam can build up and make the crust soggy.

For some pizzas, a finishing touch such as basil leaves, or a splash of a condiment is added to the pie postbake. We've marked the pizzas that require this post-cooking topping in the respective recipes so you can be clear on what to add when. Remember, basil always goes on after the pizza has come out of the oven!

TOP 10 TIPS FOR MAKING OUR ROUND PIES

1. Before stretching and shaping the dough, let it stand for at least 30 minutes at room temperature to lose its chill. The warmer the dough is, the easier it will be to shape. However, don't let it get so warm that it begins to rise.

2. Use thin pieces of fresh mozzarella for these thin-crust pies. If the mozzarella seems especially wet, let the pieces drain on kitchen towels for a few minutes.

3. For red pies, use plain crushed tomatoes (we love Jersey Fresh tomatoes cooperative). Onions, garlic, herbs, and other flavors will be added as separate ingredients, and are not cooked into the sauce. We do use Red Sauce (page 48) for some Detroit pies.

4. Spread the sauce right to the edge of the pie, with just ¼ inch (6 mm) of crust showing. We don't show a lot of crust on our pizzas and aim for these to be thin crust.

5. Preheat the oven to 525ºF (274ºC), with the pizza steel or stone in place for at least 45 minutes before adding the pizza.

6. Be sure to give the pizza on the pizza peel a good shake to be sure it is loose and not sticking to the peel. Don't wait until you get to the oven before fixing a stuck pizza.

7. For the best flavor, the upskirt (underside) of the pizza should be dotted with "leopard spots," which are darker areas with light charring. Don't be afraid of some charring on the pizza. Our ideal pie is lightly blackened around the crust edges. This isn't easy to do in a home oven, but might be accomplished if you turn the broiler on high for the last minute or so of baking.

8. If using basil, garnish the pizza with whole basil leaves. Let the guests tear the basil to add as much as they like to top each slice.

9. Cut the pizza on a cutting board, as a pizza cutter will leave marks on a wooden pizza peel surface and scratch a metal peel.

10. To keep pizza crispy longer, we serve it from a round wire mesh pizza screen set on a pizza tray. When pizza sits directly on the serving pan, trapped steam builds up and the crust will get soggy quickly. The mesh screen lifts the pizza to allow air to circulate around the pie.

ROUND PIE DOUGH (MIXER)

MAKES ENOUGH DOUGH FOR THREE 12-INCH/30.5-CM PIES (ABOUT 900 G)

Our round pie has a thin crust with a light rise. We use a combination of wheat flour for structure and rye flour for its ability to attract wild yeast and to add a light sour flavor. Be sure to add the salt after the second mix, not with the flour. Combined with 24- to 48-hour fermentation, it all adds up to outstanding pizza dough. This recipe uses a standing heavy-duty mixer, but if you don't have one, see the no-knead method on the opposite page. Please use the metric system of weighing the ingredients for this recipe (see page 46). We firmly believe in weighing the water for the best results.

¼ cup (60 ml/60 g) warm (105º to 115ºF/40ºC to 45ºC) water
¼ teaspoon (.8 g) active dry yeast or scant ¼ teaspoon (.6 g) instant
   (also called rapid-rise or bread machine) yeast
1¼ cups (300 ml/300 g) cold water
4 cups (520 g) unbleached bread flour, preferably King Arthur
1 tablespoon (10 g) rye flour
2¼ teaspoons kosher salt (7 g), preferably Diamond Crystal

1. Start the dough 24 to 48 hours before baking. Mix the warm water and yeast in the bowl of a standing heavy-duty mixer and let stand for 5 minutes. The mixture should look frothy. Add the cold water and whisk to dissolve the yeast.

2. Add the bread and rye flours. Affix the bowl to the mixer and fit with the dough hook. Mix on medium speed just until the flour is thoroughly moistened and the dough comes together into a sticky mass that cleans the sides and bottom of the bowl. Leave the hook in place and drape a kitchen towel around the open top of the bowl to cover it. Let the dough stand for about 10 minutes. (This rest period, called autolyse, allows the flour to hydrate fully before kneading.) Remove the towel.

3. Knead on medium-low speed, occasionally pulling down the dough if it climbs up the hook, until smooth and elastic, 8 to 10 minutes. The dough should be soft and sticky but still pull away from the sides of the bowl. However, when the mixer is stopped, the dough will stick to the bottom, but that is expected. Add the salt and mix until it is well distributed, about 1 minute. To check for thorough mixing, give the dough the windowpane test: Using well-floured fingers, pull off a piece about the size of a walnut. On a lightly floured surface, press it into a disc. Pick up the disc and gently pull it from all edges, working your way around the dough until it stretches into a round roughly 2 inches (5 cm) in diameter. If you can stretch the dough to this size and it is almost transparent without tearing, it has been kneaded enough. If the dough breaks, continue kneading for another minute and re-test.

4. Proceed immediately to weighing, rounding, and fermenting the dough as directed on pages 60 to 61.

ROUND PIE DOUGH (NO-KNEAD)

MAKES ENOUGH DOUGH FOR THREE 12-INCH/30.5-CM PIES (ABOUT 900 G)

For centuries, humans kneaded dough to create an invisible skeleton of gluten to give the dough structure when risen and baked. However, it was discovered that under the right conditions, it wasn't necessary to knead yeast dough, either in a mixer or by hand.

Water is required to create the gluten found in wheat flour, and if you have enough water, the gluten will strengthen on its own without kneading. In the no-knead method, we do "stretch" the dough in its mixing container every 10 minutes over a 40-minute proofing period before fermentation, which also gives the yeast a kick-start as the dough stands at room temperature. A 24-hour fermentation allows the dough to fully hydrate, develop flavor, and build strength.

You will need a 2-quart lidded container or similar bowl to mix and store the dough.

¼ cup (60 ml/60 g) warm (105º to 115ºF/40ºC to 45ºC) water
¼ teaspoon (.8 g) active dry yeast or a scant ¼ teaspoon (.6 g) instant
   (also called rapid-rise or bread machine) yeast
1¼ cups (300 ml/300 g) cold water
4 cups (520 g) unbleached bread flour, preferably King Arthur
1 tablespoon (10 g) rye flour
2¼ teaspoons (7 g) kosher salt, preferably Diamond Crystal

1. Start the dough 24 to 48 hours before baking. Mix the warm water and yeast in a 2- to 3-quart (2- to 2.8-L) lidded container or bowl. The mixture should look frothy. Whisk to dissolve the yeast. Stir in the cold water.

2. Add the bread and rye flours with the salt and stir, making sure all the flour is moistened (especially the flour lurking in the corners of the container), until it forms a shaggy mass. It will look very unpromising at this stage. Cover the container with the lid slightly ajar (or, if using a bowl, a moistened, wrung-out kitchen towel) and let stand for about 10 minutes.

3. Using wet hands, pick up the dough at its 12 o'clock position, letting the dough mass be pulled by its own weight to hang down by about 3 inches (7.5 cm). Return the dough to the container, folding the stretched portion into the center of the mass and pressing it down. Repeat the stretching and folding process for the dough's remaining three quarters at the 3, 6, and 9 o'clock positions. Cover again and let stand for about 10 minutes. Repeat the stretching, pulling, and waiting routine three more times for a total of four sessions over a 40-minute period. The dough will become smoother and less sticky with each rest.

4. Immediately proceed to weighing, shaping, and fermenting the balls of dough as directed on pages 60 to 61.

THE CLASSIC

MAKES ONE 12-INCH (30.5-CM) PIE; 6 SLICES

This is a minimalist pizza, with just sauce and fresh mozzarella. Enjoy it in its beautiful simplicity, or use it as a canvas for your favorite toppings.

> 1 ball Round Pie Dough (Mixer or No-Knead, page 68 or 69)
> ¼ cup (60 ml) canned crushed tomatoes
> ½ teaspoon dried oregano
> 4 ounces (115 g) fresh mozzarella, thinly sliced and torn into 12 pieces

1. At least 45 minutes before baking, place a baking steel or stone in the top third of the oven and preheat the oven to 525ºF (274ºC).

2. Let the pizza dough stand at room temperature, covered, for 30 to 45 minutes to lose its chill. Following the instructions on pages 62 to 65, stretch the dough into a 12-inch (30.5-cm) round. Slide the round onto a very lightly floured pizza peel and adjust the shape of the round as needed. Using the back of a large spoon, spread the tomatoes on the dough, leaving a ¼-inch (6-mm) border. Crumble and sprinkle the oregano over the crushed tomatoes. Arrange the mozzarella over the tomatoes.

3. Slide the pizza onto the steel or stone and bake until the crust is deeply browned, about 8 minutes. If you wish, during the last minute or so, change the setting to Broil/High to brown the pizza more. Using the peel, transfer the pizza to a cutting board. Using a pizza cutter, cut the pizza into sixths. Using a wide metal spatula, slide the pizza onto a pizza pan lined with a round pizza screen, or a serving platter. Serve immediately.

THE EMZIES

This pie is named for a longtime server, Emily Bolles. Since we couldn't have two Emilys running around the restaurant, Emily B. acquired Emzies as her nickname, and her pizza was born.

> 1 ball Round Pie Dough (Mixer or No-Knead, page 68 or 69)
> ¼ cup (60 ml) Tomatillo Sauce (page 50)
> ½ cup (50 g) shredded Havarti
> 2 tablespoons freshly grated pecorino Romano
> 3 ounces (85 g) sliced fresh mozzarella, torn into 9 pieces
> 8 Castelvetrano olives, pitted and halved to make 16 pieces
> 12 thin strips red onion

1. At least 45 minutes before baking, place a baking steel or stone in the top third of the oven and preheat the oven to 525ºF (274ºC).

2. Let the pizza dough stand at room temperature, covered, for 30 to 45 minutes to lose its chill. Following the instructions on pages 62 to 65, stretch the dough into a 12-inch (30.5-cm) round. Slide the round onto a very lightly floured pizza peel and adjust the shape of the round as needed. Using the back of a large spoon, spread the tomatillo sauce on the dough, leaving a ¼-inch (6-mm) border. Sprinkle with the Havarti, followed by the Romano. Top with the mozzarella. Scatter the olives and red onion over the pizza. Shake the pizza on the peel to be sure it is loose and not sticking.

3. Slide the pizza onto the steel or stone and bake until the cheese is nicely browned, about 8 minutes. If you wish, during the last minute or so, change the setting to Broil/High to brown the pizza more. Using the peel, transfer the pizza to a cutting board. Using a pizza wheel, cut the pizza into sixths. Using a wide metal spatula, slide the pizza onto a pizza pan lined with a round pizza screen, or a serving platter. Serve immediately.

THE LUCA

Luca Arrigoni, an Italian pizza maker living in Brooklyn, is the owner of Sottocasa, where Matt trained under Luca's mentoring. Our most traditionally Italian pizza is named in tribute to this amazing person. Our take on a classic Neapolitan pizza, the Luca has the traditional Margherita toppings of red tomatoes, white burrata, and green basil, with a touch of Romano and a drizzle of olive oil. This pizza, the colors of the Italian flag, is fictionally said to have been invented in 1889 to honor Queen Margherita of Savoy when she came through Naples on a state visit. Note that our pizza is topped with the delicate and creamy burrata just before serving, so the piping hot pie will warm and melt it to a just-right stage. If added sooner, it would turn into a wet and gooey mess.

> 1 ball Round Pie Dough (Mixer or No-Knead, page 68 or 69)
> ½ cup (120 ml) canned crushed tomatoes
> 2 tablespoons freshly grated pecorino Romano
> 3 ounces (85 g) burrata (about ½ of a ball)
> A handful of large fresh basil leaves, for serving
> Extra-virgin olive oil, for drizzling

1. At least 45 minutes before baking, place a baking steel or stone in the top third of the oven and preheat the oven to 525ºF (274ºC).

2. Let the pizza dough stand at room temperature, covered, for 30 to 45 minutes to lose its chill. Following the instructions on pages 62 to 65, stretch the dough into a 12-inch (30.5-cm) round. Slide the round onto a very lightly floured pizza peel and adjust the shape of the round as needed. Using the back of a large spoon, spread the tomatoes in a thin layer over the dough, leaving a ¼-inch (6-mm) border. Sprinkle with the Romano. Shake the pizza on the peel to be sure it is loose and not sticking.

3. Slide the pizza onto the steel or stone and bake until the crust is deeply browned and the sauce is bubbling, 6 to 8 minutes. If you wish, during the last minute or so, change the setting to Broil/High to brown the pizza more. Using the peel, transfer the pizza to a cutting board. Using a pizza wheel, cut the pizza into sixths. Using a wide metal spatula, slide the pizza onto a pizza pan lined with a round pizza screen, or a serving platter. Tearing the burrata into 6 roughly equal pieces, place one piece on each wedge and top with the basil. Drizzle with the olive oil and serve immediately.

THE CAMP RANDALL

MAKES ONE 12-INCH (30.5-CM) PIE; 6 SLICES

This pizza—a fan favorite—is named to honor Matt's dad. Camp Randall is the football stadium at the University of Wisconsin, where he went to school, and this hearty midwestern pie is the perfect tribute to him. What Wisconsin grad can resist a pizza slathered in cheese curds and sausage?

> 3½ ounces (100 g) hot or sweet Italian sausage, about 1 average link, casing removed
> 1 ball Round Pie Dough (Mixer or No-Knead, page 68 or 69)
> ¼ cup (60 ml) canned crushed tomatoes
> 2 tablespoons freshly grated pecorino Romano
> 10 to 12 Wisconsin Cheddar cheese curds, cut in half crosswise
> 12 thin slices green bell pepper
> 1 large cremini mushroom, stemmed and cut into ¼-inch (6-mm) slices

1. At least 45 minutes before baking, place a baking steel or stone in the top third of the oven and preheat the oven to 525°F (274°C).

2. Cook the sausage in a medium skillet over medium heat, breaking it up with the side of a spoon, until the sausage is barely cooked through but not browned, 6 to 8 minutes. Transfer to paper towels and let cool. Crumble the sausage. Set aside.

3. Let the pizza dough stand at room temperature, covered, for 30 to 45 minutes to lose its chill. Following the instructions on pages 62 to 65, stretch the dough into a 12-inch (30.5-cm) round. Slide the round onto a very lightly floured pizza peel and adjust the shape of the round as needed. Using the back of a large spoon, spread the tomatoes on the dough, leaving a ¼-inch (6-mm) border. Sprinkle the Romano on top, followed by a scattering of the Cheddar curds. Top with the green pepper, mushroom, and sausage. Shake the pizza on the peel to be sure it is loose and not sticking.

4. Slide the pizza onto the steel or stone and bake until the cheese is nicely browned, about 8 minutes. During the last minute or so, change the setting to Broil/High to brown the pizza more. Using the peel, transfer the pizza to a cutting board. Using a pizza wheel, cut the pizza into sixths. Using a wide metal spatula, slide the pizza onto a pizza pan lined with a round pizza screen, or a serving platter. Serve immediately.

THE MATT

MAKES ONE 12-INCH (30.5-CM) PIE; 6 SLICES

Matt is a particular pizza eater. His namesake pie embodies his favorite cheese: pecorino Romano, and lots of it. Starting with a bed of shredded Havarti, he adds dollops of crushed tomato and tops each with a generous sprinkle of Romano. The pie is completed with sliced creminis, making it much more than the typical mushroom pie.

1 ball Round Pie Dough (Mixer or No-Knead, page 68 or 69)
1 cup (100 g) shredded Havarti
½ cup (120 ml) canned crushed tomatoes
4 tablespoons freshly grated pecorino Romano, as needed
2 medium cremini mushrooms, stemmed and thinly sliced
Extra-virgin olive oil, for drizzling

1. At least 45 minutes before baking, place a baking steel or stone in the top third of the oven and preheat the oven to 525ºF (274ºC).

2. Let the pizza dough stand at room temperature, covered, for 30 to 45 minutes to lose its chill. Following the instructions on pages 62 to 65, stretch the dough into a 12-inch (30.5-cm) round. Slide the round onto a very lightly floured pizza peel and adjust the shape of the round as needed. Sprinkle the Havarti over the dough, leaving a ¼-inch (6-mm) border. Spoon dollops of the tomatoes all over the pizza. Sprinkle about ¼ teaspoon Romano over each dollop. Scatter the mushrooms over the topping. Shake the pizza on the peel to be sure it is loose and not sticking.

3. Slide the pizza onto the steel or stone and bake until the crust is deeply browned, about 8 minutes. If you wish, during the last minute or so, change the setting to Broil/High to brown the pizza more. Using the peel, transfer the pizza to a cutting board. Using a pizza wheel, cut the pizza into sixths. Using a wide metal spatula, slide the pizza onto a pizza pan lined with a round pizza screen, or a serving platter. Finish with a sprinkle of remaining Romano and drizzle with olive oil. Serve immediately.

THE COLONY

Of all our pizzas, this is the one that has become our most popular and most Instagrammed. It has, in our opinion, the perfect topping combination of salty, spicy, and sweet. This pizza gets its name and inspiration from the Colony Grill, an old-school (circa 1935) roadside tavern in Stamford, Connecticut, that's famous for its thin-crust pizza with hot oil.

1 ball Round Pie Dough (Mixer or No-Knead, page 68 or 69)
¼ cup (60 ml) canned crushed tomatoes
2 tablespoons freshly grated pecorino Romano
3 ounces (85 g) fresh mozzarella, thinly sliced and torn into 9 thin pieces
20 thick slices pepperoni
12 slices Pickled Jalapeños (page 209) or jarred jalapeño slices
2 tablespoons clover honey, in a plastic squeeze bottle, for drizzling

1. At least 45 minutes before baking, place a baking steel or stone in the top third of the oven and preheat the oven to 525ºF (274ºC).

2. Let the pizza dough stand at room temperature, covered, for about 30 to 45 minutes to lose its chill. Following the instructions on pages 62 to 65, stretch the dough into a 12-inch (30.5-cm) round. Slide the round onto a very lightly floured pizza peel and adjust the shape of the round as needed. Using the back of a large spoon, spread the tomatoes on the dough, leaving a ¼-inch (6-mm) border. Sprinkle with the Romano. Top with the mozzarella, then scatter the pepperoni and jalapeños on top. Shake the pizza on the peel to be sure it is loose and not sticking.

3. Slide the pizza onto the steel or stone and bake until the crust is deeply browned, about 8 minutes. If you wish, during the last minute or so, change the setting to Broil/High to brown the pizza more. Using the peel, transfer the pizza to a cutting board. Using a pizza wheel, cut the pizza into sixths. Using a wide metal spatula, slide the pizza onto a pizza pan lined with a round pizza screen, or a serving platter. Squeeze a squiggle of honey over the pizza and serve immediately.

THE MODERN

MAKES ONE 12-INCH (30.5-CM) PIE; 6 SLICES

We've named this mozzarella-less pizza for Modern Apizza, which has been in business since 1934. This is our favorite New Haven pizza spot, and we frequently hop in the car for a daytrip to the Modern. We are inspired by the best of the traditional pizzerias, but are not wedded to their methods.

1 ball Round Pie Dough (Mixer or No-Knead, page 68 or 69)
½ cup (120 ml) canned crushed tomatoes
½ teaspoon dried oregano
2 garlic cloves, finely chopped
3 tablespoons grated pecorino Romano
12 thin strips red onion
A handful of small fresh basil leaves, for serving
2 tablespoons Sichuan Oil (page 200), as needed for drizzling

1. At least 45 minutes before baking, place a baking sheet or stone in the top third of the oven and preheat the oven to 525ºF (274ºC).

2. Let the pizza dough stand at room temperature, covered, for 30 to 45 minutes to lose its chill. Following the instructions on pages 62 to 65, stretch the dough into a 12-inch (30.5-cm) round. Slide the round onto a very lightly floured pizza peel and adjust the shape of the round as needed. Using the back of a large spoon, spread the tomatoes on the dough, leaving a ¼-inch (6-mm) border. Crumble and sprinkle the oregano over the tomatoes. Top with scatterings of the garlic, the Romano, and the red onion. Shake the pizza on the peel to be sure it is loose and not sticking.

3. Slide the pizza onto the steel or stone and bake until the crust is deeply browned, about 8 minutes. If you wish, during the last minute or so, change the setting to Broil/High to brown the pizza more. Using the peel, transfer the pizza to a cutting board. Using a pizza wheel, cut the pizza into sixths. Using a wide metal spatula, slide the pizza onto a pizza pan lined with a round pizza screen, or a serving platter. Scatter the basil over the pizza and drizzle with a spiral of the Sichuan oil. Serve immediately.

THE RAFA

Building on the Round Pie, this vegetarian pizza gets kicked up a notch with green pepper and red onion. A simple yet delicious pie, it's named for Matt's childhood best friend, Rafael Vasquez, who has been an integral part of our lives, our restaurants, and our family.

> 1 ball Round Pie Dough (Mixer or No-Knead, page 68 or 69)
> ¼ cup (60 ml) canned crushed tomatoes
> ½ teaspoon dried oregano
> 4 ounces (115 g) fresh mozzarella, thinly sliced and torn into 12 pieces
> 12 thin strips green bell pepper
> 12 thin strips red onion
> A handful of small fresh basil leaves

1. At least 45 minutes before baking, place a baking steel or stone in the top third of the oven and preheat the oven to 525ºF (274ºC).

2. Let the pizza dough stand at room temperature, covered, for 30 to 45 minutes to lose its chill. Following the instructions on pages 62 to 65, stretch the dough into a 12-inch (30.5-cm) round. Slide the round onto a very lightly floured pizza peel and adjust the shape of the round as needed. Using the back of a large spoon, spread the tomatoes on the dough, leaving a ¼-inch (6-mm) border. Crumble and sprinkle the oregano on the tomatoes. Arrange the mozzarella evenly on top, followed by the bell pepper and red onion. Shake the pizza on the peel to be sure it is loose and not sticking.

3. Slide the pizza onto the steel or stone and bake until the crust is deeply browned, about 8 minutes. If you wish, during the last minute or so, change the setting to Broil/High to brown the pizza more. Using the peel, transfer the pizza to a cutting board. Using a pizza wheel, cut the pizza into sixths. Using a wide metal spatula, slide the pizza onto a pizza pan lined with a round pizza screen, or a serving platter. Top with the basil leaves and serve immediately.

THE RED PLANET

MAKES ONE 12-INCH (30.5-CM) PIE; 6 SLICES

This red pie is named after our favorite planet. We have vegan guests who love this pizza because it was created to be dairy-free, and they don't have to ask for any special tweaks. It's proof that you don't have to load a pizza with cheese for it to be tasty. An extra helping of crushed tomatoes ensures that it's red enough to earn its name.

1 ball Round Pie Dough (Mixer or No-Knead, page 68 or 69)
½ cup (120 ml) canned crushed tomatoes
½ teaspoon dried oregano
2 garlic cloves, finely chopped
A handful of small fresh basil leaves, for serving
Extra-virgin olive oil, for drizzling

1. At least 45 minutes before baking, place a baking steel or stone in the top third of the oven and preheat the oven to 525ºF (274ºC).

2. Let the pizza dough stand at room temperature, covered, for 30 to 45 minutes to lose its chill. Following the instructions on pages 62 to 65, stretch the dough into a 12-inch (30.5-cm) round. Slide the round onto a very lightly floured pizza peel and adjust the shape of the round as needed. Using the back of a large spoon, spread the tomatoes on the dough, leaving a ¼-inch (6-mm) border. Crumble and sprinkle the oregano on top, followed with a scattering of the garlic. Shake the pizza on the peel to be sure it is loose and not sticking.

3. Slide the pizza onto the steel or stone and bake until the crust is deeply browned, about 8 minutes. If you wish, during the last minute or so, change the setting to Broil/High to brown the pizza more. Using the peel, transfer the pizza to a cutting board. Using a pizza wheel, cut the pizza into sixths. Using a wide metal spatula, slide the pizza onto a pizza pan lined with a round pizza screen, or a serving platter. Scatter the basil over the pizza and finish with a drizzle of olive oil on top. Serve immediately.

THE RM3

Raymond Musalo III, Matt's cousin, is extremely proud of this pizza—the name is also an acronym for "Real Meaty Three." If you're so inclined, substitute diced smoked ham for the bacon. Just remember not to load the top too heavily with the meat, or you'll weigh down the thin crust and it will be difficult to slide into the oven.

3½ ounces (100 g) hot or sweet Italian sausage, about 1 average-sized link, casing removed

1 slice thick-cut applewood-smoked bacon, cut crosswise into sixths

1 ball Round Pie Dough (Mixer or No-Knead, page 68 or 69)

¼ cup (60 ml) canned crushed tomatoes

2 tablespoons freshly grated pecorino Romano

1 cup (100 g) shredded Havarti

12 thin slices pepperoni

1. At least 45 minutes before baking, place a baking steel or stone in the top third of the oven and preheat the oven to 525ºF (274ºC).

2. Cook the sausage in a medium skillet over medium heat, breaking up the meat with the side of a spoon, until it is barely cooked through but not browned, 4 to 6 minutes. Using a slotted spoon, transfer to paper towels and let cool. Crumble the sausage. Discard the fat.

3. Add the bacon to the skillet and cook over medium heat, stirring occasionally, until it is translucent and heated through but not crisp and browned, 6 to 8 minutes. Using the slotted spoon, transfer the bacon to the paper towels and let cool. Discard the fat.

4. Let the pizza dough stand at room temperature, covered, for 30 to 45 minutes to lose its chill. Following the instructions on pages 62 to 65, stretch the dough into a 12-inch (30.5-cm) round. Slide the round onto a very lightly floured pizza peel and adjust the shape of the round as needed. Using the back of a large spoon, spread the tomatoes on the dough, leaving a ¼-inch (6-mm) border. Sprinkle with the Romano, followed by the Havarti. Scatter the sausage, bacon, and pepperoni on top. Shake the pizza on the peel to be sure it is loose and not sticking.

5. Slide the pizza onto the steel or stone and bake until the crust is deeply browned, about 8 minutes. If you wish, during the last minute or so, change the setting to Broil/High to brown the pizza more. Using the peel, transfer the pizza to a cutting board. Using a pizza wheel, cut the pizza into sixths. Using a wide metal spatula, slide the pizza onto a pizza pan lined with a round pizza screen, or a serving platter. Serve immediately.

THE WILLIAM

MAKES ONE 12-INCH (30.5-CM) PIE; 6 SLICES

Our nephew William was born so close to our opening date that we felt it was only fair to name a pizza after him. And so we did, adding some of our favorite flavor-packed toppings. The William is a neighborhood favorite, just as William, the kiddo, is a personal favorite to Auntie Em and Uncle Matt. We love you, William!

1 ball Round Pie Dough (Mixer or No-Knead, page 68 or 69)
¼ cup (60 ml) canned crushed tomatoes
2 tablespoons freshly grated pecorino Romano
½ teaspoon dried oregano
1 garlic clove, finely chopped
4 ounces (115 g) fresh mozzarella, thinly sliced and torn into 12 pieces
8 Castelvetrano olives, pitted and halved
12 thin strips red onion
A handful of small fresh basil leaves

1. At least 45 minutes before baking, place a baking steel or stone in the top third of the oven and preheat the oven to 525ºF (274ºC).

2. Let the pizza dough stand at room temperature, covered, for 30 to 45 minutes to lose its chill. Following the instructions on pages 62 to 65, stretch the dough into a 12-inch (30.5-cm) round. Slide the round onto a very lightly floured pizza peel and adjust the shape of the round as needed. Using the back of a large spoon, spread the tomatoes on the dough, leaving a ¼-inch (6-mm) border. Sprinkle with the Romano, followed by the oregano and garlic. Arrange the mozzarella evenly over the top and add the olives and red onion. Shake the pizza on the peel to be sure it is loose and not sticking.

3. Slide the pizza onto the steel or stone and bake until the crust is deeply browned, about 8 minutes. If you wish, during the last minute or so, change the setting to Broil/High to brown the pizza more. Using the peel, transfer the pizza to a cutting board. Using a pizza wheel, cut the pizza into sixths. Using a wide metal spatula, slide the pizza onto a pizza pan lined with a round pizza screen, or a serving platter. Top with the basil leaves and serve immediately.

THE WRESTLER

The Wrestler is composed of Matt's all-time-favorite trio of toppings: pepperoni, mushrooms, and olives. He shares this favorite combination with Emily's cousin Russell, whom Matt has nicknamed "The Wrestler" as a play on his name in pizza form.

1 ball Round Pie Dough (Mixer or No-Knead, page 68 or 69)
¼ cup (60 ml) canned crushed tomatoes
½ teaspoon dried oregano
4 ounces (115 g) fresh mozzarella, thinly sliced and torn into 12 pieces
1 large shiitake mushroom, stemmed and thinly sliced
8 Castelvetrano olives, pitted and halved
16 thin slices pepperoni

1. At least 45 minutes before baking, place a baking steel or stone in the top third of the oven and preheat the oven to 525ºF (274ºC).

2. Let the pizza dough stand at room temperature, covered, for 30 to 45 minutes to lose its chill. Following the instructions on pages 62 to 65, stretch the dough into a 12-inch (30.5-cm) round. Slide the round onto a very lightly floured pizza peel and adjust the shape of the round as needed. Using the back of a large spoon, spread the tomatoes on the dough, leaving a ¼-inch (6-mm) border. Crumble and sprinkle the oregano on the tomatoes. Arrange the mozzarella evenly over the top. Top with the mushroom, olives, and pepperoni. Shake the pizza on the peel to be sure it is loose and not sticking.

3. Slide the pizza onto the steel or stone and bake until the crust is deeply browned, about 8 minutes. If you wish, during the last minute or so, change the setting to Broil/High to brown the pizza more. Using the peel, transfer the pizza to a cutting board. Using a pizza wheel, cut the pizza into sixths. Using a wide metal spatula, slide the pizza onto a pizza pan lined with a round pizza screen, or a serving platter. Serve immediately.

THE EMILY

MAKES ONE 12-INCH (30.5-CM) PIE; 6 SLICES

This pie originated because Emily loves eating cheese with honey; naturally, Matt honored her favorite pairing on this signature pie. Like dessert for dinner, crumbled pistachios, drizzled honey, and truffle cheese make for an indulgent and unique offering whether your dinner guests are named "Emily" or not.

> 1 ball Round Pie Dough (Mixer or No-Knead, page 68 or 69)
> 2 tablespoons freshly grated pecorino Romano
> 3 ounces (85 g) fresh mozzarella, thinly sliced and torn into 9 pieces
> ⅓ cup (35 g) shredded Havarti
> 2 tablespoons coarsely chopped pistachios
> 2 tablespoons clover honey, as needed, in a plastic squeeze bottle
> ⅓ cup (35 g) freshly shredded sottocenere or other truffle-flavored cheese
> Extra-virgin olive oil, for drizzling

1. At least 45 minutes before baking, place a baking steel or stone in the top third of the oven and preheat the oven to 525ºF (274ºC).

2. Let the pizza dough stand at room temperature, covered, for 30 to 45 minutes to lose its chill. Following the instructions on pages 62 to 65, stretch the dough into a 12-inch (30.5-cm) round. Slide the round onto a very lightly floured pizza peel and adjust the shape of the round as needed. Sprinkle with the Romano. Top with the mozzarella pieces and use the Havarti to fill in the blank areas on the pizza. Shake the pizza on the peel to be sure it is loose and not sticking.

3. Slide the pizza onto the steel or stone and bake until the cheese is nicely browned, about 8 minutes. If you wish, during the last minute or so, change the setting to Broil/High to brown the pizza more. Using the peel, transfer the pizza to a cutting board. Using a pizza wheel, cut the pizza into sixths. Using a wide metal spatula, slide the pizza onto a pizza pan lined with a round pizza screen, or a serving platter. Sprinkle with the pistachios. Working from edge to edge, squeeze a thin spiral of honey over the pizza. Top with the sottocenere. Drizzle with the oil and serve immediately.

THE LADY PIZZA GIRL

MAKES ONE 12-INCH (30.5-CM) PIE; 6 SLICES

Our guests are familiar with the smiling face of our cartoon mascot, the triangular Lady Pizza Girl. There is a real pizza girl in our world, Emily's sister, and her name is Lauren. She is one of the hard-working people who helped us open in Clinton Hill in 2014 by stretching pizza dough by Matt's side on a nightly basis. In appreciation, this one is for you, Lady Pizza Girl.

> 1 ball Classic Round Pie Dough (Mixer or No-Knead, page 68 or 69)
> 2 tablespoons freshly grated pecorino Romano
> ¼ cup (50 g) Fresh Ricotta (page 208) or store-bought ricotta
> ½ cup (50 g) shredded Havarti
> 12 slices Pickled Jalapeños (page 209) or bottled jalapeño slices
> 1 large shiitake mushroom, stemmed and thinly sliced
> ½ teaspoon dried oregano
> A handful of small fresh basil leaves

1. At least 45 minutes before baking, place a baking steel or stone in the top third of the oven and preheat the oven to 525ºF (274ºC).

2. Let the pizza dough stand at room temperature, covered, for 30 to 45 minutes to lose its chill. Following the instructions on pages 62 to 65, stretch the dough into a 12-inch (30.5-cm) round. Slide the round onto a very lightly floured pizza peel and adjust the shape of the round as needed. Sprinkle with the Romano. Top with about 8 dollops of ricotta. Sprinkle the Havarti on the pizza, filling in the gaps between the ricotta dollops. Add the jalapeño and mushroom slices. Crumble and sprinkle the oregano on top. Shake the pizza on the peel to be sure it is loose and not sticking.

3. Slide the pizza onto the steel or stone and bake until the cheese is nicely browned, about 8 minutes. If you wish, during the last minute or so, change the setting to Broil/High to brown the pizza more. Using the peel, transfer the pizza to a cutting board. Using a pizza wheel, cut the pizza into sixths. Using a wide metal spatula, slide the pizza onto a pizza pan lined with a round pizza screen, or a serving platter. Top with the basil and serve immediately.

THE DUNE ROAD

MAKES TWO 12-INCH (30.5-CM) PIES; 12 SLICES

Named for the long stretching thruway along the beach where Matt spent his summers in Westhampton, this pie evokes the pleasure of fresh seafood from the market and takeout from Johnny Chih's. Littleneck or cherrystone clams are the best choice here because they are the right size and tenderness for baking in a hot oven. (Note that this makes two pizzas because it's difficult to make a smaller amount of the sauce.)

CLAMS AND SAUCE

1 cup (240 ml) dry white wine

24 littleneck clams, scrubbed, soaked in salty water for 1 hour, and drained

1 tablespoon unsalted butter

1 tablespoon unbleached all-purpose flour

3 tablespoons heavy cream

1 tablespoon ssamjang

½ teaspoon fish sauce, preferably Three Crabs brand

2 balls Round Pie Dough (Mixer or No-Knead, page 68 or 69)

4 tablespoons (25 g) freshly grated pecorino Romano

2 tablespoons Sichuan Oil (page 200)

12 fresh basil leaves, for serving

1. To prepare the clams: Bring the wine to a boil in a large nonreactive saucepan. Add the clams and cover tightly. Cook, occasionally shaking the skillet, until all of the clams open, about 6 minutes. Use kitchen tongs to transfer the clams to a large bowl as they open. Set the clams aside to cool.

2. Line a wire sieve with a double layer of rinsed-out cheesecloth or paper towels and place the sieve over a bowl. Strain the cooking liquid through the sieve, leaving any grit behind in the saucepan. Measure and reserve ½ cup (120 ml) of the cooking juice and discard the rest. (Or save the juice to use as seafood stock in another recipe.) Set aside. Remove the clam meat from the shells, discarding the shells. Transfer the clam meat to a lidded container, cover, and refrigerate until ready to use or up to 1 day.

3. To make the sauce: Melt the butter in a small saucepan over medium-low heat. Whisk in the flour and let it bubble without browning for 1 minute. Whisk in the reserved cooking juice and cream and bring to a simmer. Cook, whisking often, until lightly thickened, about 3 minutes. Whisk in the ssamjang and fish sauce, return to a simmer, and cook for about 2 minutes more to blend the flavors. Remove from the heat and let cool completely. Transfer to a lidded container, cover, and refrigerate until the sauce is chilled, at least 1 hour or up to 1 day.

4. At least 45 minutes before baking, place a baking steel or stone in the top third of the oven and preheat the oven to 525ºF (274ºC).

5. Let the pizza dough stand at room temperature, covered, for 30 to 45 minutes to lose its chill. Following the instructions on pages 62 to 65, stretch 1 ball of the dough into a 12-inch (30.5-cm) round. Slide the round onto a very lightly floured pizza peel and adjust the shape of the round as needed. Stir the chilled sauce well to loosen it. Using the back of a large spoon, spread half of the sauce over the pizza, leaving a ¼-inch (6-mm) border around the edges. Scatter 12 clams onto the pizza and sprinkle with 2 tablespoons of the Romano.

6. Slide the pizza onto the steel or stone and bake until the crust is deeply browned and the sauce is bubbling, about 8 minutes. During the last minute or so of baking, switch the thermostat to Broil/High to brown the pizza more. Using the peel, remove the pizza from the oven and slide it onto a cutting board. Using a pizza wheel, cut the pizza into sixths. Using a wide metal spatula, transfer the pizza onto a pizza pan lined with a round pizza screen, or a serving platter. Drizzle a spiral of about 1 tablespoon of the Sichuan oil over the pizza and top with half of the basil leaves. Serve immediately.

7. To make the second pizza, repeat and bake with the remaining ingredients.

ABOUT KOREAN PASTES

Korean cuisine leans heavily on an array of amazingly flavorful seasoning pastes. Just a tablespoon or two can really wake up a dish.

Jang means "sauce" in Korean, making it easier to identify the pastes at the supermarket. We use *gochujang* (chili paste) and *ssamjang* (a spicy, salty condiment used as a dip) at the restaurants, but you can also find two other kinds of *jang: doenjang* (a chunky cousin to Japanese miso) and *chunjang* (a black bean noodle sauce).

Each paste is always sold in a color-coded plastic tub or clear glass jar: Gochujang is in a red container, ssamjang is green, doenjang is brown or dark beige, and chunjang is black. Covered and refrigerated in their containers, they will keep for months and months.

Gochujang, a thick and sticky fermented chili paste, is an iconic ingredient in Korean cooking. The chile used in gochujang has a slightly sweet, raisin-like undertone similar to the ancho chile in Mexican cooking. Gochujang comes in an array of spice levels; we prefer medium for our recipes.

Ssamjang is based on the miso-like doenjang and is seasoned with chiles, garlic, and other tasty ingredients. This sauce is the essential condiment for *ssam* (which means "wrapped" in Korean), a communal meal of sliced pork and other fillings rolled up in edible leaves such as lettuce, perilla, or shiso.

THE NORTH MAPLE

MAKES ONE 12-INCH (30.5-CM) PIE; 6 SLICES

We're open for weekend lunch, so we offer a few breakfast-inspired pizzas to ease our guests' reentry into the day. This one, named for the street Matt grew up on, is reminiscent of New England mornings with the combination of bacon, warm pecans, and maple syrup wafting through the kitchen.

> 1 slice thick-cut applewood-smoked bacon, cut into 6 lengths
> 1 ball Round Pie Dough (Mixer or No-Knead, page 68 or 69)
> 2 tablespoons freshly grated pecorino Romano
> ½ cup (50 g) shredded Havarti
> 2 ounces (55 g) thinly sliced fresh mozzarella, torn into 6 pieces
> 2 tablespoons coarsely chopped pecans
> 2 tablespoons pure maple syrup, as needed, for drizzling

1. At least 45 minutes before baking, place a baking steel or stone in the top third of the oven and preheat the oven to 525ºF (274ºC).

2. Cook the bacon in a large skillet over medium heat, stirring occasionally, until it is barely cooked through but not browned, 4 to 6 minutes. (The bacon will be cooked more in the oven, so don't brown it at this point or it can overcook.) Transfer the bacon to paper towels to drain and cool.

3. Let the pizza dough stand at room temperature, covered, for 30 to 45 minutes to lose its chill. Following the instructions on pages 62 to 65, stretch the dough into a 12-inch (30.5-cm) round. Slide the round onto a very lightly floured pizza peel and adjust the shape of the round as needed. Sprinkle with the Romano, followed by the Havarti. Top with the mozzarella and bacon. Shake the pizza on the peel to be sure it is loose and not sticking.

4. Slide the pizza onto the steel and bake until the toppings are golden brown, about 8 minutes. If you wish, during the last minute or so, change the setting to Broil/High to brown the pizza more. Using the peel, transfer the pizza to a cutting board. Using a pizza wheel, cut the pizza into sixths. Using a wide metal spatula, slide the pizza onto a pizza pan lined with a round pizza screen, or a serving platter. Sprinkle the pecans on top. Drizzle a spiral of maple syrup over the pizza and serve immediately.

THE QUINN

Eight-year-old Quinn, pizza artist extraordinaire and the sister of Fancy Phoebe commemorated on page 186, has been coming to the Brooklyn restaurant since the week we opened our doors. As one of our most dedicated regular guests, it was fitting that she entered our pizza name pantheon with her own pie, an all-cheese number.

> 1 ball Round Pie Dough (Mixer or No-Knead, page 68 or 69)
> 2 tablespoons freshly grated pecorino Romano
> ½ cup (50 g) shredded Havarti
> 3 ounces (85 g) fresh mozzarella, thinly sliced and torn into about
>   9 pieces
> 3 tablespoons Fresh Ricotta (page 208) or store-bought ricotta

1. At least 45 minutes before baking, place a baking steel or stone in the top third of the oven and preheat the oven to 525ºF (274ºC).

2. Let the pizza dough stand at room temperature, covered, for 30 to 45 minutes to lose its chill. Following the instructions on pages 62 to 65, stretch the dough into a 12-inch (30.5-cm) round. Slide the round onto a very lightly floured pizza peel and adjust the shape of the round as needed. Sprinkle with the Romano, followed by the Havarti. Top with the mozzarella pieces and add dollops of the ricotta. Shake the pizza on the peel to be sure it is loose and not sticking.

3. Slide the pizza onto the steel or stone and bake until the cheese is nicely browned, about 8 minutes. If you wish, during the last minute or so, change the setting to Broil/High to brown the pizza more. Using the peel, transfer the pizza to a cutting board. Using a pizza wheel, cut the pizza into sixths. Using a wide metal spatula, slide the pizza onto a pizza pan lined with a round pizza screen, or a serving platter. Serve immediately.

THE SUBURBAN HANGOVER

MAKES ONE 12-INCH (30.5-CM) PIE; 6 SLICES

We all know that the best cure for a hangover is a bacon, egg, and cheese sandwich on a round roll with salt, pepper, and ketchup. This sandwich was pivotal to our weekend mornings when we were building out the Clinton Hill restaurant. As a pizza, this combo is even better! To keep the egg topping from overcooking, we partially bake the pizza for a couple of minutes, then pop the egg on top. You could also fry the egg separately in a skillet to your desired doneness and slip it onto the pizza just before serving. To keep the yolk from running all over, cut the pizza on the serving pan at the table.

> 1 slice thick-cut applewood-smoked bacon, cut crosswise into sixths
> 1 ball Round Pie Dough (Mixer or No-Knead, page 68 or 69)
> 2 tablespoons freshly grated pecorino Romano
> 3 ounces (85 g) fresh mozzarella, thinly sliced and torn into about
>   9 pieces
> 1 large egg
> Freshly ground black pepper
> Ketchup, for serving (optional)

1. At least 45 minutes before baking, place a baking steel or stone in the top third of the oven and preheat the oven to 525ºF (274ºC).

2. Cook the bacon in a large skillet over medium heat, stirring occasionally, until it is barely cooked through but not browned, 4 to 6 minutes. (The bacon will be cooked more in the oven, so don't brown it at this point or it can overcook.) Transfer the bacon to paper towels to drain and cool.

3. Let the pizza dough stand at room temperature, covered, for 15 to 30 minutes. Following the instructions on pages 62 to 65, stretch the dough into a 12-inch (30.5-cm) round. Slide the round onto a very lightly floured pizza peel and adjust the shape of the round as needed. Sprinkle with the Romano. Add the mozzarella, but leave an empty space in the center to contain the egg. Shake the pizza on the peel to be sure it is loose and not sticking.

4. Slide the pizza onto the steel and bake until the dough looks set but not browned, about 3 minutes. If you wish, during the last minute or so, change the setting to Broil/High to brown the pizza more. Using the peel, remove the pizza from the oven. Crack the egg into the center. Carefully return the pizza to the oven, taking care not to shake it too much and dislodge the egg. (It helps to set the far edge of the pizza on the steel, then use your free thumb to push the pizza off the peel.) Bake until the cheese is nicely browned, about 8 minutes. Transfer the pizza to a pizza pan lined with a round pizza screen, or a serving platter. Grind pepper over the egg to taste. Serve immediately with a serrated knife (such as a steak knife) for cutting at the table, and ketchup, if you wish.

THE UNCLE RAY

MAKES ONE 12-INCH (30.5-CM) PIE; 6 SLICES

We probably don't have to tell you that Matt's Uncle Ray likes a white pizza with character, so here he is in unique pizza form. He is Emily's backgammon rival of over a decade; the man is unbeatable, no matter how many hours she plays against him on Christmas Day. This pie is in honor of his reign as champion.

> 1 ball Round Pie Dough (Mixer or No-Knead, page 68 or 69)
> 2 tablespoons grated pecorino Romano
> ½ cup (50 g) shredded Havarti
> 3 ounces (85 g) thin slices fresh mozzarella, torn into about 9 pieces
> 3 tablespoons Fresh Ricotta (page 208) or store-bought ricotta
> ½ cup cubed (½-inch/12-mm) smoked ham, about 2½ ounces (70 g)
> 2 tablespoons Sichuan Oil (page 200)

1. At least 45 minutes before baking, place a baking steel or stone in the top third of the oven and preheat the oven to 525ºF (274ºC).

2. Let the pizza dough stand at room temperature, covered, for 30 to 45 minutes to lose its chill. Following the instructions on pages 62 to 65, stretch the dough into a 12-inch (30-cm) round. Slide the round onto a very lightly floured pizza peel and adjust the shape of the round as needed. Sprinkle with the Romano, followed by the Havarti. Top with the mozzarella pieces, add dollops of the ricotta, and evenly scatter the ham over all. Shake the pizza on the peel to be sure it is loose and not sticking.

3. Slide the pizza onto the steel or stone and bake until the cheese is nicely browned, about 8 minutes. If you wish, during the last minute or so, change the setting to Broil/High to brown the pizza a little more. Using the peel, transfer the pizza to a cutting board. Using a pizza wheel, cut the pizza into sixths. Using a wide metal spatula, slide the pizza onto a pizza pan lined with a round pizza screen, or a serving platter. Starting at the center of the pie, drizzle a spiral of the Sichuan oil on top. Serve immediately.

#EMMYEATS

You won't find this super-savory pie on the menu, but we'll be happy to make it for you upon request. Emily would probably put her beloved ranch dressing on chocolate cake if we let her, so the ranch finish marks the pizza as her invention. Unlike so many pizzerias, we do not sprinkle oregano on everything, but its aroma and taste are just right here, blending with other bold ingredients like banana peppers and red onion.

> 1 ball Round Pie Dough (Mixer or No-Knead, page 68 or 69)
> ¼ cup (60 ml) Vodka Sauce (page 49)
> ½ cup (50 g) shredded Havarti
> 2 tablespoons freshly grated pecorino Romano
> 3 ounces (85 g) fresh mozzarella, thinly sliced and torn into 9 pieces
> ½ teaspoon dried oregano
> 12 slices pickled banana peppers, drained on paper towels
> 12 thin strips red onion
> 2 tablespoons Chive Ranch Dressing (page 199), in a plastic squeeze bottle

1. At least 45 minutes before baking, place a baking steel or stone in the top third of the oven and preheat the oven to 525ºF (274ºC).

2. Let the pizza dough stand at room temperature, covered, for 30 to 45 minutes to lose its chill. Following the instructions on pages 62 to 65, stretch the dough into a 12-inch (30.5-cm) round. Slide the round onto a very lightly floured pizza peel and adjust the shape of the round as needed. Using the back of a large spoon, spread the vodka sauce on the dough, leaving a ¼-inch (6-mm) border. Sprinkle with the Havarti, followed by the Romano. Top with the mozzarella. Crumble and sprinkle the oregano over all. Add the banana peppers and red onion strips. Shake the pizza on the peel to be sure it is loose and not sticking.

3. Slide the pizza onto the steel or stone and bake until the cheese is nicely browned, about 8 minutes. If you wish, during the last minute or so, change the setting to Broil/High to brown the pizza more. Using the peel, transfer the pizza to a cutting board. Using a pizza wheel, cut the pizza into sixths. Using a wide metal spatula, slide the pizza onto a pizza pan lined with a round pizza screen, or a serving platter. Squeeze a large hashtag pattern of ranch dressing on the pizza and serve immediately.

THE ¡MADRE!

We have sipped a few mezcals in our time at El Atoradero and Madre, our favorite Mexican restaurant/bar, situated in Brooklyn's Prospect Heights. The pairing of chorizo and salsa verde is one of our favorite flavor combinations in the Mexican tradition. We use soft, fresh Mexican chorizo here, and not the hard, smoked-link Spanish variety. However, if you can't get your hands on the soft kind, you can substitute about a dozen thin slices of the hard chorizo, which does not need precooking.

> 3½ ounces (100 g) fresh Mexican chorizo, about 1 average link, casing removed
> 1 ball Round Pie Dough (Mixer or No-Knead, page 68 or 69)
> 2 tablespoons freshly grated pecorino Romano
> ½ cup (50 g) shredded Havarti
> 3 ounces (85 g) fresh mozzarella, thinly sliced and torn into 9 pieces
> 3 tablespoons Tomatillo Sauce (page 50), in a plastic squeeze bottle

1. At least 45 minutes before baking, place a baking steel or stone in the top third of the oven and preheat the oven to 525ºF (274ºC).

2. Cook the chorizo in a medium skillet over medium heat, breaking up the chorizo with the side of a spoon, until it is just cooked through but not browned, 6 to 8 minutes. (The chorizo will cook more in the oven, so don't brown it at this point or it could burn later.) Transfer to paper towels and let cool. Crumble the chorizo. Set aside.

3. Let the pizza dough stand at room temperature, covered, for 30 to 45 minutes to lose its chill. Following the instructions on pages 62 to 65, stretch the dough into a 12-inch (30.5-cm) round. Slide the round onto a very lightly floured pizza peel and adjust the shape of the round as needed. Sprinkle with the Romano, followed by the Havarti. Top with the mozzarella. Shake the pizza on the peel to be sure it is loose and not sticking.

4. Slide the pizza onto the steel and bake until the cheese is nicely browned, about 8 minutes. If you wish, during the last minute or so, change the setting to Broil/High to brown the pizza more. Using the peel, transfer the pizza to a cutting board. Using a pizza wheel, cut the pizza into sixths. Using a wide metal spatula, slide the pizza onto a pizza pan lined with a round pizza screen, or a serving platter. Starting at the center of the pizza, squeeze a spiral of tomatillo sauce on top. Serve immediately.

CHAPTER 5

DETROIT PIES

Though we love our round, wood-fired pies, we have a long history of ordering square pies to eat on the couch and watch cartoons. So, when opening our new location, we knew we wanted to cook square pies in pans; through research, we quickly learned that we were making what is called "Detroit-Style Pizza." A true Detroit pizza will be rectangular, lightly puffed, and topped with lots of sauce and cheese. And, the best part about this type of pizza is that there is extra cheese sprinkled around the perimeter of the pan. When cooking, the cheese fries around the edges to create a crispy, crunchy cheese-crust known as *frico,* a term brought into contemporary pizza dialogue by pizza expert Adam Kuban.

Based on its shape you may think you recognize this pie as a Grandma or Sicilian pizza, but the Detroit has its own set of rules, including the type of baking pan, where to put the sauce, and the kind of (domestic) cheese used. Get ready to have a new favorite pizza.

MAKING OUR DETROIT PIES

When making our Detroit pies, we strive for a number of key qualities that you might aim to achieve as well: We cook the pizza in an 8 x 10 (20 x 25 cm) rectangular pan, and we try for a crispy bottom, crunchy-cheese crust, airy middle, lots of cheese, hearty toppings, and two stripes of sauce down the length of the pie. We find Detroit pies to be really accessible and lots of fun for pizza parties, especially with kiddos.

The Right Pans: The story goes that workers at automobile manufacturers in Detroit were given deep blue-steel utility trays to hold nuts, lugs, and other necessary car parts at their stations. Some adventuresome worker discovered that they were a good size for baking the Detroit pie at home. Because of the pans dark color and heavy gauge, the cheese that touched the pan walls got toasted and crisp. This is the irresistible frico crust that separates a Detroit-style pie from any old pan pizza.

You can find authentic, black metal Detroit-style pizza pans online. The old blue steel ones are virtually impossible to find. Today's authentic Detroit pan comes with a snap-on plastic lid to keep the dough surface from drying out.

Purists are going to insist on these dark, heavy metal pans, and if you're a pan

purist, more power to you. Knowing that not everyone is going to want to invest in a special pan, we tried a few substitutes, and the results were great. The typical Detroit pizza pan measures 8 x 11 inches (20 x 28 cm), and shiny metal baking pans with the exact same dimensions are readily available. The common supermarket oblong pan—or brownie pan—measures 7 x 11 inches (17 x 28 cm) and works very well. If it has a dark nonstick surface, you'll get browning power similar to the dark metal "original." You can use either of these pans with confidence. A plastic wrap topping, secured in place with rubber bands (to prevent it slipping off in the fridge) is a workable solution for a plastic pan top. Whatever kind of pan you purchase, follow the manufacturer's instructions for cleaning.

Make and Ferment the Dough: Follow the recipes for either the mixer or no-knead versions of the Detroit pie dough on page 104 or 105. Either recipe makes three balls of dough for three 11-x-7-inch (28-x-17-cm) pizzas. Let the dough ferment in bulk in the refrigerator for 24 to 36 hours.

Weigh the Dough: Using a bowl scraper, scrape the dough out of the bowl onto a lightly floured work surface. Weigh the dough; it should be about 900 grams. Divide the number by three to get the exact weight for each ball. Using the bench knife, cut the dough into thirds.

Weigh each third on a kitchen scale, trimming and adding bits of dough from each ball as needed to get the right amount. Each ball should weigh about 300 grams. Remember that there will be a little dough left in the bowl and on the spoon, so the weights will vary by a few grams one way or the other. Do not stress out over it.

Pan the Dough: Pat the three portions into three buttered pans (see above). If you aren't using a well-seasoned black metal Detroit pizza pan, a nonstick rectangular pan (see opposite page) is a great second choice.

Proof the Dough: Cover each pan with plastic wrap (or the plastic lid of a Detroit-pizza pan) and secure it in place with rubber bands at the opposite ends. Let the dough proof (rise) at room temperature until the dough looks slightly puffy but not doubled, about 1½ hours.

Refrigerate the Dough: Place the dough in the refrigerator to chill for at least 2 or up to 36 hours before using. The dough must be chilled before topping.

Top the Dough: Because the dough is baked in the pan, the topping procedure is not as delicate as it is for round pizzas, but there are some tips.

The frico is formed by a mixture of mild Cheddar and mozzarella, two cheeses known for their ability to melt beautifully. Be sure to apply most of the shredded mixture around the edges of the dough so it comes into contact with the sides of the pan to make the frico edge. This will ensure that the cheese melts into the desired crispy state. The remainder of the cheese is scattered over the exposed center of the dough.

The main thing to remember about a Detroit pie is that the cheese goes on first and the sauce afterward. The typical method is to spoon the sauce in two thick strips (about 1 inch/2.5 cm wide and about 1 inch/2.5 cm apart) running lengthwise over the cheese and leaving a 1-inch (2.5-cm) border on all four sides.

For other toppings, distribute them so they are spaced evenly across the top crust. The pizza will be cut into sixths, so be sure that each piece has some of the topping ingredients.

Bake the Pizza: As with round pizzas, preheat the oven for at least 45 minutes at 525ºF (274ºC). If you have a baking steel or stone, use it; this will help brown the bottom of the crust. We bake our Detroit pies in a convection oven, which circulates air around the pan and encourages better browning of the sides and the formation of the frico. If you have a convection oven, preheat it to 500ºF (260ºC) and reduce the baking time by about 3 minutes.

Serve the Pizza: The crisp, browned edges of the pizza (the frico) can stick to the pan. Allow the pie to stand at room temperature for a minute or two after it comes out of the oven so it can pull away slightly from the pan. Use a bench knife or a small sharp knife, if necessary, to cut through the frico and loosen the pizza.

Slip a bench knife or a wide metal spatula under the pizza and slide the pizza onto a cutting board. Use a pizza wheel to slice the pie into sixths, and garnish as the recipe instructs with any finishing touches such as sauce, honey, or basil.

TOP 10 TIPS FOR OUR DETROIT PIES

1. Sprinkle the shredded Cheddar/mozzarella mixture generously at the dough border on all four sides, making sure the cheese touches the pan sides so it can melt and brown to form the crisp frico edges during baking.

2. Utilize low-moisture mozzarella, the classic topping for American-style Detroit pies.

3. Sauces for Detroit pies are always applied *over* the cheese topping, not under it. This is the easiest way to spoon two long, wide strips of sauce running lengthwise over the cheese.

4. Detroit pies use the robust red sauce on page 48, not plain crushed tomatoes.

5. Don't tense up about what kind of rectangular pan to use. If you don't have a dark metal classic Detroit pan, use a nonstick oblong baking pan (about 7 x 11 inches/ 17 x 28 cm) instead.

6. Use softened unsalted butter to generously grease the pans. The milk solids in the butter will encourage a deeper browning of the crust better than oil.

7. Be sure the dough is well chilled before adding the toppings. If the dough is warm or at room temperature, it could collapse under the weight of the ingredients.

8. You will get better bottom browning of the crust if the baking pan sits on a baking steel or stone.

9. Let the pizza cool for a minute or so before attempting to remove it from the pan. If you didn't use a nonstick pan, a small sharp knife may be needed to cut the crisp frico away from the pan sides.

10. Always remove the pizza from the pan before serving. A wide spatula is a helpful tool at this moment. Slice the pizza before moving it to a rectangular wire rack set over a serving plate or pan.

DETROIT PIE DOUGH (MIXER)

ENOUGH DOUGH FOR THREE 11 X 7-INCH/28 X 17-CM PIES (ABOUT 900 G)

For our Detroit-inspired pizzas, we use a somewhat puffy, porous dough reminiscent of focaccia or Sicilian pizza. To achieve this, we add oil and extra yeast to the dough. As with the Round Pie Dough (page 68), start a day early so the dough can rise and develop flavor. The dough is refrigerated in bulk for 1 to 2 days, pressed into buttered pans, allowed to proof for an hour or so, then chilled for another couple of hours (or up to 1 day) before baking. Please use the metric system of weighing the ingredients for this recipe (see page 40). We firmly believe in weighing the water for the best results.

¼ cup (60 ml/60 g) warm (105° to 115°F/40° to 45°C) water

1 teaspoon (4 g) sugar

1 teaspoon (3.2 g) active dry yeast or 1 scant teaspoon (2.8 g) instant (also called rapid-rise or bread machine) yeast

1¼ cups (300 ml/300 g) cold water

4 cups plus 1 tablespoon (530 g) unbleached bread flour, preferably King Arthur

1½ tablespoons (22 ml) canola or vegetable oil, plus more for the bowl

2¼ teaspoons (7 g) kosher salt, preferably Diamond Crystal

1. Start the dough 24 to 48 hours before baking. Mix the warm water, sugar, and yeast in the bowl of a standing heavy-duty mixer and let stand for 5 minutes. The mixture should look frothy. Add the cold water.

2. Add the flour. Affix the bowl to the mixer and fit with the dough hook. Mix on medium speed just until the dough comes together. Leave the hook in place and drape a kitchen towel around the open top of the bowl to cover it. Let the dough stand for about 10 minutes. (This rest period, called autolyse, allows the flour to hydrate fully before kneading.) Remove the towel.

3. Knead on medium-low speed, occasionally pulling down the dough if it climbs up the hook, until smooth, elastic, and passes the windowpane test (see page 68), 6 to 8 minutes. The dough should be soft and sticky but still pull away from the sides of the bowl. Increase the speed to medium-high. Drizzle in the oil, mixing until it is absorbed, about 2 minutes. (If the dough doesn't come together, increase the mixer speed a notch or two.) Add the salt and mix until it is well distributed.

4. Tightly cover with the lid (or, if using a bowl, with plastic wrap) and refrigerate to ferment for 24 to 48 hours. After this period, the dough can be transferred to pans for its final proof and chilling as directed on page 101.

DETROIT PIE DOUGH (NO-KNEAD)

Here is the low-tech, handmade, no-knead version of our light-textured Detroit pie dough. While the ingredient measurements are the same, the mixing process is entirely different. Keep this sequence in mind when preparing the dough: Bulk ferment for 1 to 2 days, press into buttered pans and proof for about an hour, then chill in the pans for another couple of hours (or up to 1 day) before baking.

¼ cup (60 ml/60 g) warm (105º to 115ºF/40º to 45ºC) water

1 teaspoon (4 g) sugar

1 teaspoon (3.2 g) active dry yeast or 1 scant teaspoon (2.8 g) instant (also called rapid-rise or bread machine) yeast

1¼ cups (300 ml/300 g) cold water

1½ tablespoons (22 ml) canola or vegetable oil

4 cups plus 1 tablespoon (530 g) unbleached bread flour, preferably King Arthur

2¼ teaspoons (7 g) kosher salt, preferably Diamond Crystal

1. Start the dough 24 to 48 hours before baking. Mix the warm water, sugar, and yeast in a 2- to 3-quart (2- to 2.8-L) lidded container or large bowl. Let stand until the mixture looks frothy, about 5 minutes. Add the cold water and oil and whisk to thoroughly dissolve the yeast.

2. Add the flour and salt and stir, making sure all of the flour is moistened (especially the flour lurking in the corners of the container), until it forms a shaggy mass. It will look very unpromising at this stage. Cover the container with the lid slightly ajar (or, if using a bowl, a moistened, wrung-out kitchen towel) and let stand for about 10 minutes.

3. Using wet hands, pick up the dough at its 12 o'clock position, letting the dough mass stretch by its own weight and hang down by about 3 inches (7.5 cm). (Give it a shake to help it along, if needed.) Return the dough to the container, folding the stretched portion into the center of the mass and pressing it down. Repeat the stretching and folding process of the dough's remaining three quarters at the 3, 6, and 9 o'clock positions. Cover again and let stand for about 10 minutes. Repeat the stretching, pulling action three more times for a total of four sessions over a 40 minute period. The dough will get smoother and less sticky with each rest.

4. Tightly cover with the lid (or, if using a bowl, with plastic wrap) and refrigerate to ferment for 24 to 48 hours. After this period, the dough can be transferred to pans for its final proof and chilling as directed on page 101.

THE GRAMMY

MAKES 1 DETROIT PIE; 6 PIECES

Grandma is one of our children—I mean cats, and her nickname is Grammy. She is an uncomplicated lady, and we think she would like her namesake pizza to be very simple, too. All the Grammy pizza requires is red sauce and the classic cheese combination.

1 pan Detroit Pie Dough (Mixer or No-Knead, page 104 or 105), chilled
½ cup (50 g) shredded mild Cheddar
½ cup (50 g) shredded low-moisture mozzarella
6 tablespoons (90 ml) Red Sauce (page 48)
2 tablespoons freshly grated pecorino Romano

1. At least 45 minutes before baking, place a baking steel or stone in the top third of the oven and preheat the oven to 525ºF (274ºC).

2. Uncover the dough in the pan. Mix the Cheddar and mozzarella together. Sprinkle about two-thirds of the cheese heavily around the edges of the pan and evenly scatter the remainder in the central section of the dough. Using 3 tablespoons red sauce for each, spoon two strips, each about 1½ inches (4 cm) wide and 1 inch (2.5 cm) apart on the pizza, leaving a 1-inch (2.5-cm) border on all four sides. Sprinkle with the Romano.

3. Place the pan onto the steel or stone in your oven and bake until the top of the pie is golden brown with crisp edges, about 10 minutes. Remove the pan from the oven and let stand for about 1 minute. Using a small sharp knife, loosen the pizza around all four sides. Using a wide metal spatula, transfer the pizza to a cutting board. Using a pizza wheel, cut the pizza into sixths. Slip the spatula under the pizza and move it to a small rimmed baking sheet (quarter-sheet pan) lined with a rectangular wire rack, or a serving platter. Serve immediately.

THE MIMI

Mimi Cheng's Dumplings is a wonderful bastion of juicy Taiwanese dumplings in Manhattan. We have a symbiotic relationship with the owners, sisters Hannah and Marian Cheng: We love their dumplings; they love our pizza. They even invented an EMMY dumpling with beef and onions, based on our burger. To reciprocate with a Mimi pizza, we asked them for their favorite pizza combination—and here it is.

1 pan Detroit Pie Dough (Mixer or No-Knead, page 104 or 105), chilled
½ cup (50 g) shredded mild Cheddar
½ cup (50 g) low-moisture mozzarella
½ cup (120 ml) Red Sauce (page 48)
3 tablespoons Fresh Ricotta (page 208) or store-bought ricotta
2 teaspoons puréed Garlic Confit (page 207)
1 large shiitake mushroom, stemmed and thinly sliced
2 tablespoons freshly grated pecorino Romano
A handful of small fresh basil leaves, for serving

1. At least 45 minutes before baking, place a baking steel or stone in the top third of the oven and preheat the oven to 525ºF (274ºC).

2. Uncover the dough in the pan. Mix the Cheddar and mozzarella together. Sprinkle about two-thirds of the cheese heavily around the edges of the pan and evenly scatter the remainder in the central section of the dough. Using 3 tablespoons of red sauce for each, spoon two strips, each about 1½ inches (4 cm) wide and 1 inch (2.5 m) apart on the pizza, leaving a 1-inch (2.5-cm) border on all four sides. Top with dollops of the ricotta and garlic confit. Scatter the mushroom slices over the top and sprinkle with the Romano.

3. Place the pan onto the steel or stone in your oven and bake until the top of the pie is golden brown with crisp edges, about 10 minutes. Remove the pan from the oven and let stand for about 1 minute. Using a small sharp knife, loosen the pizza around all four sides. Using a wide metal spatula, transfer the pizza to a cutting board. Using a pizza wheel, cut the pizza into sixths. Slip the spatula under the pizza and move it to a small rimmed baking sheet (quarter-sheet pan) lined with a rectangular wire rack, or a serving platter. Scatter the basil on top and serve immediately.

FOR THE NGUYEN

MAKES 1 DETROIT PIE; 6 PIECES

This is a shout-out to our friend Tim Nguyen, who created many inspired dishes at our original, Clinton Hill location. To keep the meat from drying out in the hot oven, we simmer juicy chicken thighs in a Japanese braising mixture. The intensely flavored Nguyen sauce is a great finishing touch.

POACHED CHICKEN
1 cup (240 ml) water
1 cup (240 ml) okonomiyaki sauce
1 chicken thigh with skin and bone, about 6 ounces (170 g)

1 pan Detroit Pie Dough (Mixer or No-Knead, page 104 or 105), chilled
½ cup (50 g) shredded mild Cheddar
½ cup (50 g) shredded low-moisture mozzarella
3 tablespoons crumbled blue cheese
½ scallion, white and pale green parts, sliced
2 tablespoons freshly grated pecorino Romano
1 tablespoon Nguyen Sauce (page 198), as needed
6 paper-thin radish slices, preferably breakfast or French radish cut
    lengthwise on a mandoline or V-slicer

1. To cook the chicken: Whisk the water and okonomiyaki sauce together in a small saucepan. Add the chicken and bring to a boil over medium heat. Reduce the heat to medium-low and cover the saucepan with the lid ajar. Simmer for about 20 minutes. Remove from the heat and let the chicken cool in the liquid, about 30 minutes. Remove from the liquid and pull the meat into shreds, discarding the skin and bones. Reserve the chicken meat and discard the poaching liquid.

2. At least 45 minutes before baking, place a baking steel or stone in the top third of the oven and preheat the oven to 525ºF (274ºC).

3. Uncover the dough in the pan. Mix the Cheddar and mozzarella together. Sprinkle about two-thirds of the cheese mixture heavily around the edges of the pan and evenly scatter the remainder in the central section of the dough. Sprinkle with the blue cheese, followed by the chicken, scallion, and Romano.

4. Place the pan onto the steel or stone in your oven and bake until the top of the pie is golden brown with crisp edges, about 10 minutes. Do not worry if the scallions are charred, as this will add to the flavor. Remove the pan from the oven and let stand for about 1 minute. Using a small sharp knife, loosen the pizza around all

four sides. Using a wide metal spatula, transfer the pizza to a cutting board. Using a pizza wheel, cut the pizza into sixths. Slip the spatula under the pizza and transfer it to a small rimmed baking sheet (quarter-sheet pan) lined with a rectangular wire rack, or a serving platter. Drizzle with a light zigzag of the Nguyen sauce. Top each piece with a radish slice and serve immediately.

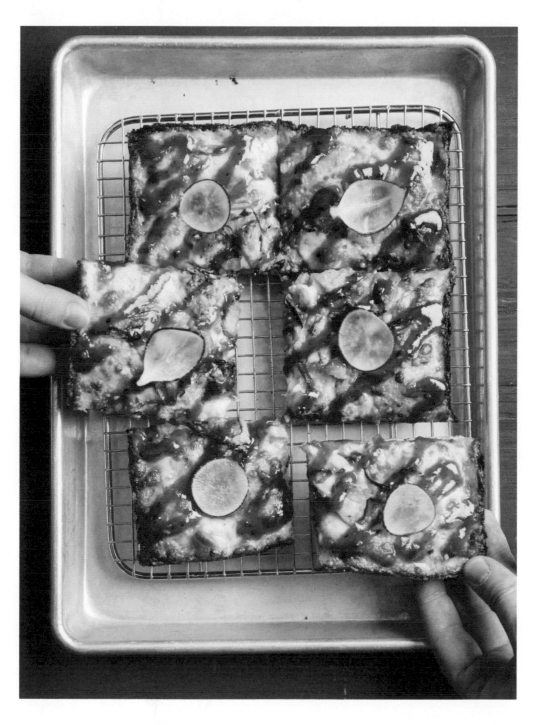

THE GOODS

MAKES 1 DETROIT PIE; 6 PIECES

Named after our resident comedian, Alyson Goodman, who is another founding staff member from the original location, this pie is a deconstructed version of our EMMY burger in pizza form. This pie is a secret, off-menu item that is sometimes available, so ask for it when you dine with us or, even better, just try this recipe out at home whenever you want!

1 pan Detroit Pie Dough (Mixer or No-Knead, page 104 or 105), chilled

½ cup (50 g) shredded mild Cheddar

½ cup (50 g) low-moisture mozzarella

1 slice American cheese

3 tablespoons Caramelized Onions (page 206)

¼ teaspoon kosher salt

4 ounces (115 g) ground chuck (15 percent fat) beef

2 tablespoons freshly grated pecorino Romano

6 slices bread-and-butter pickles

¼ cup (60 ml) EMMY Sauce (page 125), preferably in a squeeze bottle, as needed for serving

1. At least 45 minutes before baking, place a baking steel or stone in the top third of the oven and preheat the oven to 525ºF (274ºC).

2. Uncover the dough in the pan. Mix the Cheddar and mozzarella together. Sprinkle about two-thirds of the cheese mixture heavily around the edges of the pan and evenly scatter the remainder in the central section of the dough. Tear the American cheese into 3 or 4 pieces and scatter over the pie. Leaving a 1-inch (2.5-cm) border on all sides, sprinkle the caramelized onions over the pizza.

3. Salt the beef and break into little pieces on top of the pizza. Sprinkle with the Romano.

4. Place the pan onto the steel or stone in your oven and bake until the top of the pie is golden brown with crisp edges, about 10 minutes. Remove from the oven and let stand for about 1 minute. Using a small sharp knife, loosen the pizza around all four sides. Using a wide metal spatula, transfer the pizza to a cutting board. Cut the pizza into sixths. Place a pickle on the center top of each piece. Slip the spatula under the pizza and move to a small rimmed baking sheet (quarter-sheet pan) lined with a rectangular wire rack, or a serving platter. Squeeze the EMMY sauce in a zigzag pattern over the top of the pizza and serve immediately.

THE STREET FAIR

MAKES 1 DETROIT PIE; 6 PIECES

In New York, we have a lot of street fairs, where blocks, or entire neighborhoods, are closed off for a day of fun and food. This pizza is an homage to the delicious sausage sandwiches that are the highlight of going to a NYC street fair.

> 3½ ounces (100 g) hot or sweet Italian sausage, about 1 average-sized link, casing removed
> 1 pan Detroit Pie Dough (Mixer or No-Knead, page 104 or 105), chilled
> ½ cup (50 g) shredded mild Cheddar
> ½ cup (50 g) shredded low-moisture mozzarella
> 1 thinly sliced red onion, cut in half crosswise and separated into strips
> 2 pickled red cherry peppers, cut crosswise into rounds and excess seeds discarded, drained on paper towels
> 2 tablespoons freshly grated pecorino Romano

1. At least 45 minutes before baking, place a baking steel or stone in the top third of the oven and preheat the oven to 525ºF (274ºC).

2. Cook the sausage in a medium skillet over medium heat, breaking up the meat with the side of a spoon, until it is barely cooked through but not browned, 6 to 8 minutes. Transfer to paper towels and let cool. Crumble the sausage and set aside.

3. Uncover the dough in the pan. Mix the Cheddar and mozzarella together. Sprinkle about two-thirds of the cheese mixture heavily around the edges of the pan and evenly scatter the remainder in the central section of the dough. Leaving a 1-inch (2.5-cm) border on all four sides, sprinkle the red onion over the pizza, followed by the cherry peppers and sausage. Sprinkle with the Romano.

4. Place the pan onto the steel or stone in your oven and bake until the top of the pie is golden brown with crisp edges, about 10 minutes. Remove the pan from the oven and let stand for about 1 minute. Using a small sharp knife, loosen the pizza around all four sides. Using a wide metal spatula, transfer the pizza to a cutting board. Using a pizza wheel, cut the pizza into sixths. Slip the spatula under the pizza and move it to a small rimmed baking sheet (quarter-sheet pan) lined with a rectangular wire rack, or a serving platter. Serve immediately.

THE PIG FREAKER

MAKES 1 DETROIT PIE; 6 PIECES

Pig Bleecker is a restaurant around the corner from our West Village location. We are friendly with the owners, and we love their food. We invented this meaty pizza as a tribute to them! If you don't have scallion kimchi, you can certainly use your favorite store-bought version.

1 slice thick-cut applewood-smoked bacon, cut into 1-inch (2.5-cm) lengths

1 pan Detroit Pie Dough (Mixer or No-Knead, page 104 or 105), chilled

½ cup (50 g) shredded mild Cheddar

½ cup (50g) shredded low-moisture mozzarella

2 tablespoons freshly grated pecorino Romano

⅓ cup (80 g) Scallion Kimchi (page 204) or store-bought kimchi

½ teaspoon black sesame seeds

½ teaspoon white sesame seeds

3 tablespoons Miso Queso (page 203), as needed

1. At least 45 minutes before baking, place a baking steel or stone in the top third of the oven and preheat the oven to 525ºF (274ºC).

2. Cook the bacon in a large skillet over medium heat, stirring occasionally, until translucent and heated through but not crisp and browned, 4 to 6 minutes. (The bacon will be cooked more in the oven, so don't brown it at this point or it can overcook.) Transfer the bacon to paper towels to drain and cool.

3. Uncover the dough in the pan. Mix the Cheddar and mozzarella together. Sprinkle about two-thirds of the cheese mixture heavily around the edges of the pan, and evenly scatter the remainder in the central section of the dough. Sprinkle with the Romano, followed by the bacon.

4. Place the pan onto the steel or stone in your oven and bake until the top of the pie is golden brown with crisp edges, about 10 minutes. Remove the pan from the oven and let stand for about 1 minute. Using a small sharp knife, loosen the pizza around all four sides. Using a wide metal spatula, transfer the pizza to a cutting board. Using a pizza wheel, cut the pizza into sixths. Slip the spatula under the pizza and move it to a small rimmed baking sheet (quarter-sheet pan) lined with a rectangular wire rack, or a serving platter. Top with the kimchi and sprinkle with the black and white sesame seeds. Drizzle the miso queso over the pizza. Serve immediately.

THE WHITEOUT

MAKES 1 DETROIT PIE; 6 PIECES

If you are the kind of person who values a grilled sandwich lusciously oozing with melted cheese, then this pizza is for you. Because of the selection of cheeses used here, the pie has a slightly sharper flavor than, say, the round Quinn, with its mild mozzarella and ricotta.

> 1 pan Detroit Pie Dough (Mixer or No-Knead, page 104 or 105), chilled
> ¼ cup (25 g) shredded mild Cheddar
> ¼ cup (25 g) shredded low-moisture mozzarella
> ¼ cup (25 g) shredded Appenzeller or Gruyère
> ¼ cup (25 g) shredded sharp Cheddar, preferably farmhouse style
> 3 tablespoons Fresh Ricotta (page 208) or store-bought ricotta
> 2 tablespoons freshly grated pecorino Romano

1. At least 45 minutes before baking, place a baking steel or stone in the top third of the oven and preheat the oven to 525ºF (274ºC).

2. Uncover the dough in the pan. Mix the mild Cheddar and mozzarella together. Sprinkle the cheese mixture heavily around the edges of the pan. Sprinkle the Appenzeller and sharp Cheddar evenly in the central section of the dough. Top with dollops of the ricotta. Sprinkle with the Romano.

3. Place the pan onto the steel or stone in your oven and bake until the top of the pie is golden brown with crisp edges, about 10 minutes. Remove the pan from the oven and let stand for about 1 minute. Using a small sharp knife, loosen the pizza around all four sides. Using a wide metal spatula, transfer the pizza to a cutting board. Using a pizza wheel, cut the pizza into sixths. Slip the spatula under the pizza and move it to a small rimmed baking sheet (quarter-sheet pan) lined with a rectangular wire rack, or a serving platter. Serve immediately.

THE VODKA

This pie has only a few ingredients; all the better to appreciate the rich vodka sauce and beautifully fragrant basil. A perfect base for adding your own favorite toppings.

1 pan Detroit Pie Dough (Mixer or No-Knead, page 104 or 105), chilled
½ cup (50 g) shredded mild Cheddar
½ cup (50 g) shredded low-moisture mozzarella
6 tablespoons (90 ml) Vodka Sauce (page 49)
2 tablespoons freshly grated pecorino Romano
A handful of small fresh basil leaves, for serving

1. At least 45 minutes before baking, place a baking steel or stone in the top third of the oven and preheat the oven to 525ºF (274ºC).

2. Uncover the dough in the pan. Mix the Cheddar and mozzarella together. Sprinkle about two-thirds of the cheese mixture heavily around the edges of the pan, and evenly scatter the remainder in the middle of the dough. Using 3 tablespoons of vodka sauce for each, spoon two strips, each about 1½ inches (4 cm) wide and 1 inch (2.5 cm) apart, on the pizza, leaving a 1-inch (2.5-cm) border on all four sides. Sprinkle with the Romano.

3. Place the pan onto the steel or stone in your oven and bake until the top of the pie is golden brown with crisp edges, about 10 minutes. Remove the pan from the oven and let stand for about 1 minute. Using a small sharp knife, loosen the pizza around all four sides. Using a wide metal spatula, transfer the pizza to a cutting board. Using a pizza wheel, cut the pizza into sixths. Slip the spatula under the pizza and move it to a small rimmed baking sheet (quarter-sheet pan) lined with a rectangular wire rack, or a serving platter. Scatter the basil on top and serve immediately.

THE ARENSTEIN

MAKES 1 DETROIT PIE; 6 PIECES

Our friend and fellow restaurateur Noah Arenstein came up with this variation on the round Colony by asking for vodka sauce instead of red sauce. When we opened the West Village location, we morphed this from a round pie into a Detroit pie. You could use the Red Sauce (page 48) to create a Detroit pie version of the Colony. Noah won't mind.

> 1 pan Detroit Pie Dough (Mixer or No-Knead, page 104 or 105), chilled
> ½ cup (50 g) shredded mild Cheddar
> ½ cup (50 g) shredded low-moisture mozzarella
> ½ cup (120 ml) Vodka Sauce (page 49)
> 20 slices pepperoni
> 12 slices Pickled Jalapeños (page 209) or store-bought sliced jalapeños for nachos
> 2 tablespoons freshly grated pecorino Romano
> 2 tablespoons honey, in a plastic squeeze bottle, as needed

1. At least 45 minutes before baking, place a baking steel or stone in the top third of the oven and preheat the oven to 525ºF (274ºC).

2. Uncover the dough in the pan. Mix the Cheddar and mozzarella together. Sprinkle about two-thirds of the cheese heavily around the edges of the pan and evenly scatter the remainder in the central section of the dough. Spoon the vodka sauce in two strips, each about 1½ inches (4 cm) wide, and 1 inch (2.5 cm) apart on the pizza, leaving a 1-inch (2.5-cm) border on all four sides. Arrange the pepperoni in rows on top and scatter the jalapeño slices over the pepperoni. Sprinkle with the Romano.

3. Place the pan onto the steel or stone in your oven and bake until the top of the pie is golden brown with crisp edges, about 10 minutes. Remove the pan from the oven and let stand for about 1 minute. Using a small sharp knife, loosen the pizza around all four sides. Using a wide metal spatula, transfer the pizza to a cutting board. Using a pizza wheel, cut the pizza into sixths. Slip the spatula under the pizza and move it to a small rimmed baking sheet (quarter-sheet pan) lined with a rectangular wire rack or a serving platter. Squeeze a zigzag of honey over the pizza and serve immediately.

THE QUATTRO

MAKES 1 DETROIT PIE; 6 PIECES

There is a long lineage of men named Ray in Matt's family, and this pizza is named for the most recent addition, Ray IV. For the times when you can't decide between tomatillo and ranch dressing on your pizza, this pie, named after the cutest of kiddos, has both.

> 1 slice thick-cut applewood-smoked bacon, cut into 1-inch (2.5-cm) lengths
>
> 1 pan Detroit Pie Dough (Mixer or No-Knead, page 104 or 105), chilled
>
> ½ cup (50 g) shredded mild Cheddar
>
> ½ cup (50 g) shredded low-moisture mozzarella
>
> 10 slices Pickled Jalapeños (page 209) or store-bought sliced jalapeños for nachos
>
> 2 tablespoons freshly grated pecorino Romano
>
> 3 tablespoons Chive Ranch Dressing (page 199), in a plastic squeeze bottle
>
> 3 tablespoons Tomatillo Sauce (page 50), in a plastic squeeze bottle

1. At least 45 minutes before baking, place a baking steel or stone in the top third of the oven and preheat the oven to 525ºF (274ºC).

2. Cook the bacon in a large skillet over medium heat, stirring occasionally, until translucent and heated through but not crisp and browned, 6 to 8 minutes. (The bacon will be cooked more in the oven, so don't brown it at this point or it can overcook.) Transfer the bacon to paper towels to drain and cool.

3. Uncover the dough in the pan. Mix the Cheddar and mozzarella together. Sprinkle about two-thirds of the cheese mixture heavily around the edges of the pan and evenly scatter the remainder in the central section of the dough. Top with the bacon and jalapeño slices, distributing them evenly. Sprinkle with the Romano.

4. Place the pan onto the steel or stone in your oven and bake until the top of the pie is golden brown with crisp edges, about 10 minutes. Remove the pan from the oven and let stand for about 1 minute. Using a small sharp knife, loosen the pizza around all four sides. Using a wide metal spatula, transfer the pizza to a cutting board. Using a pizza wheel cut the pizza into sixths. Slip the spatula under the pizza and move it to a small rimmed baking sheet (quarter-sheet pan) lined with a rectangular wire rack, or a serving platter. Squeeze a zigzag of ranch dressing over the pizza and repeat with the tomatillo sauce. Serve immediately.

THE JERRIER

MAKES 1 DETROIT PIE; 6 PIECES

This pizza is named after Jay Jerrier, of Cane Rosso Pizza in Texas. Ranch dressing is taboo at his establishment, so as a friendly dig, Emily and Matt developed his namesake pie and covered it with ranch. Even though he bans ranch, we adore him and his family because they founded and run a dog rescue, Cane Rosso Rescue, which is dear to our hearts. Please check out their site to help save some puppies: canerossorescue.com.

> 1 pan Detroit Pie Dough (Mixer or No-Knead, page 104 or 105), chilled
> ½ cup (50 g) shredded mild Cheddar
> ½ cup (50 g) shredded low-moisture mozzarella
> 6 tablespoons (90 ml) Vodka Sauce (page 49)
> 2 thin half-moons red onion, separated into individual strips
> 2 pickled red cherry peppers, cut crosswise into rounds and excess seeds discarded, drained on paper towels
> 2 tablespoons freshly grated pecorino Romano
> 2 tablespoons Chive Ranch Dressing (page 199), in a plastic squeeze bottle, as needed

1. At least 45 minutes before baking, place a baking steel or stone in the top third of the oven and preheat the oven to 525ºF (274ºC).

2. Uncover the dough in the pan. Mix the Cheddar and mozzarella together. Sprinkle about two-thirds of the cheese mixture heavily around the edges of the pan and evenly scatter the remainder in the central section of the dough. Using 3 tablespoons of vodka sauce for each, spoon two strips, each about 1½ inches (4 cm) wide and 1 inch (2.5 cm) apart, on the pizza, leaving a 1-inch (2.5-cm) border on all four sides. Scatter the red onion strips and cherry peppers on top. Sprinkle with the Romano.

3. Place the pan onto the steel or stone in your oven and bake until the top of the pie is golden brown with crisp edges, about 10 minutes. Remove the pan from the oven and let stand for about 1 minute. Using a small sharp knife, loosen the pizza around all four sides. Using a wide metal spatula, transfer the pizza to a cutting board. Using a pizza wheel, cut the pizza into sixths. Slip the spatula under the pizza and move it to a small rimmed baking sheet (quarter-sheet pan) lined with a rectangular wire rack, or a serving platter. Squeeze a zigzag of ranch dressing over the pizza. Serve immediately.

@pizzalovesfamily

CHAPTER 6

THE EMMY
BURGER

When you open a pizza restaurant, you do so because you fundamentally love eating pizza. That, at least, is the reason Matt and I opened EMILY. And when you open a pizza restaurant and are working every day, all day, all you have time to eat is pizza. And while I will never tire of eating pizza every day (and still eat it many times a week), somewhere in the early summer of 2014, Matt had had enough. He needed to eat something else. And, since he is the owner and the chef, he decided to create a burger for the menu that was exactly what he wanted to eat. He has called me "Emmy" as a pet name for as long as I can remember, so I was touched when the affectionate naming of menu items continued and he coined his creation "The EMMY Burger."

Since then, this burger to beat all burgers has been on countless "best of New York" lists. It only goes to show how a chef can start with a simple concept, but can make it something extraordinary by adding his or her expertise.

The original EMMY Burger was much different than the one it is today. It had a thick cut of charred onion and was on a pan au lait bun served on a butcher board. Matt would make the burgers for family meals and send the burger out to regulars to gauge interest and garner feedback. Of course, as the burger evolved and Matt turned the thick cut of onions into buttery caramelized onions, chose to use high-end dry-aged beef, carefully picked Grafton cheddar as the cheese-topping winner, slathered the creation with EMMY Sauce, and placed it on a pretzel bun, the burger that he had made so as to eat something besides pizza in the back kitchen quickly became the burger that changed the trajectory of our lives.

By the fall of 2014, we were selling EMMY burgers regularly but struggling to handle the volume. By nature, the original EMILY kitchen, tiny as a shoebox, is designed to do high volumes of pizza, but we never expected to do high volumes of much else. To handle the burgers, we had to buy a new fridge just for burger meat, since our walk-in was too tiny, and hire a new addition to what had been a one-man line. We wound up capping the availability of EMMY Burgers to "25 a night," trucking along to fill the requests.

I have always loved to doodle and draw cartoons for Matt. He has boxes and books of cartoons I have made for him over the years. Since EMILY opened, I had been drawing a little pizza dude for him in various journals. As we had recently moved the burger onto a metal tray with paper underneath it to evoke the nostalgia of a fast-food archetype, I thought it would be sweet to create a doodle for the paper on which Matt's burger would sit. So, I drew the pizza-burger dude (see page 120). Then, I had a beloved regular and talented graphic designer named Chris Nguyen, who eats her fair share of Nguyen sauce, digitize the dude so I could make the paper. When it arrived, I felt it was the perfect tribute I was able to make to honor Matt's beloved burger. People loved the whole package and started coming right when we opened to sit at the bar and snag a burger before we sold out, and word started to spread.

Then, in the winter of 2015, The Infatuation wrote the most humbling and heart-warming review we have ever received, and they hollered to the New York food scene that people must eat our burger. It became burger mania at EMILY after that. Yes, people still of course came for our pizzas, but we forever became known for the EMMY Burger, and our lives truly changed. Our little mom-and-pop passion project suddenly had lines down the block and around the corner forty-five minutes before dinner service. Our host would get scoffed at angrily when she had to tell guests we were out of burgers. The burger Matt made out of a want for something different to eat provided us the opportunity to build a true future in the difficult world of the restaurant industry.

I hope that you enjoy making your own home versions of this dish that is so close and beloved to us both. Matt's hard-and-fast rule is that the pretzel bun is the best bun, so I implore you to make your own (recipe on page 210) or hunt those down rather than settle for the easy-grab potato bun at the supermarket. And re-member, like all of our condiments, EMMY sauce is certainly not meant only for burgers. It is an excellent dipping sauce for fries and pizza crusts as well.

ABOUT DRY-AGED BEEF

At EMILY in Clinton Hill, our burger is composed of dry-aged beef. We prefer this style of beef because it has a strong, intense, and earthy flavor profile, which when combined with all of the other toppings on this burger makes for an incredibly rich and unique taste experience. Dry-aging beef is a complex process that evaporates excess moisture from the meat, thereby intensifying and improving the flavor. We encourage you to seek out a high-quality, local butcher to procure meat for your burger, and we emphasize sourcing beef that is traceable and responsibly raised.

As he is for many other restaurants in New York, Pat LaFrieda is our butcher. His company provides us with the dry-aged beef we use for the EMMY burgers along with all other meats we use in-house.

Should you be so inclined, the good news is that you can grind and mix beef at home, too, for great burgers that are close to the one we serve at EMILY. There are many choices for meat grinders. You can go old school with an inexpensive hand-crank model. Or you can buy a food grinder attachment for your standing heavy-duty mixer, such as a KitchenAid. If you think you're going to grind a lot of meat, purchase a moderately priced electric grinder. You can even do a good job using your food processor by pulsing the meat in small batches.

No matter what appliance you choose, it is imperative to use ice-cold, even partially frozen, meat. During grinding, the friction will heat up the meat, which causes the fat to soften and melt into the meat, making a greasy-tasting burger. To get the meat properly cold, cut the beef into pieces about 1-inch (2.5-cm) square and freeze them until they are partially solid, about 1 hour.

It is also imperative to freeze all of the working parts of the meat grinder. This step is often overlooked, and it makes all the difference in the world. Remember, you want to do everything you can to keep the fat cold and distinct. For your at-home burger, we suggest you grind an 80 percent meat with 20 percent fat blend of your favorite cuts.

BURGER TIPS

• Never overhandle ground beef, or your burgers might become tough. Just press the meat together enough to help it hold its shape.

• Season the burger with pepper just before adding the cheese. The heat from the burger will release the pepper's oils. If you season with pepper before placing the burgers on the grill, the pepper could burn and taste acrid. However, you can season the outside of the burger with salt, because the salt isn't subject to burning.

• We purposely cook the burger rare and then let it stand to finish cooking with residual heat to medium-rare. The rest period helps distribute the heat and juices more evenly for a moist, perfectly cooked patty with an appetizing red-pink center.

• During the resting period, the burger must be placed on a wire rack set on a rimmed baking sheet to catch any drips, which should be minimal. You want air to circulate all around the patty so the heat distributes evenly. If the burger rests directly on a plate, steam will collect on the underside, increasing the chance that this area could be overcooked.

• We can't emphasize enough the importance of a high-quality burger bun. Not everyone has access to the Tom Cat Pretzel Bun we love, but there are certainly alternatives. Many bakeries make brioche buns, a good substitute. A hot burger requires a warm bun! Please take the time to toast and butter the bread before building your burger.

THE EMMY BURGER

Here it is: the recipe for the EMMY Burger. Look carefully at the ingredients, and you'll see a collection of umami-rich foods that combine into mouthful after mouthful of lusciousness. We're also providing a variation, the two-patty EMMY Double-Stack Burger, for those who can handle the challenge. You could serve the burgers with fries and cornichons, just like we do at our original Clinton Hill location.

EMMY SAUCE
½ cup (120 ml) mayonnaise
¼ cup (60 ml) Nguyen Sauce (page 198)

BURGERS
28 ounces (800 g) dry-aged burger meat or substitute with your favorite cut
Kosher salt and freshly ground black pepper
4 slices (¼ inch/6 mm thick) sharp white Cheddar, preferably Grafton Village, about 3 ounces (85 g) total
4 Pretzel Buns (page 210) or high-quality store-bought rolls, split crosswise
2 tablespoons unsalted butter, at room temperature, for spreading
Caramelized Onions (page 206), warmed as desired

Special equipment: Hand-cranked or electric meat grinder, or a food processor

1. To make the sauce: Mix the mayonnaise and Nguyen sauce together in a small bowl. Cover and refrigerate until ready to use.

2. To make the burgers from scratch: Cut the meat into 1-inch (6-mm) chunks. Freeze meat until cold or slightly frozen, about 1 hour. Freeze the meat grinder parts, or processor bowl and blade, at the same time.

3. Using a meat grinder or food processor (see page 123), coarsely grind the semifrozen meat, letting it fall into a medium bowl. (If using a food processor, pulse the meat in small batches and transfer it to a medium bowl.) Handling the ground beef gently, shape it into four rounds, each about 4 inches (10 cm) wide and ¾ inch (2 cm) thick.

4. Heat a large griddle or skillet, preferably cast iron, over medium-high heat. Heavily season the burgers on both sides with salt. Place on the pan. Cook for 2½ minutes, adjusting the heat so the underside of the patty is browning steadily but not burning. Turn the patty, season with pepper, and top with a slice of Cheddar cheese. Continue cooking for another 2½ minutes. Press the burger on top with a finger; it should feel only slightly firm. If you want to use an instant-read thermometer to check for doneness, insert the probe through the side into the center of the burger; it should read 120ºF (48ºC) for rare. Transfer the patties to a wire rack set on a large rimmed baking sheet (half-sheet pan) and let stand for 3 to 5 minutes. The internal temperature will rise a few more degrees during the rest period.

5. Meanwhile, wipe the excess fat from the griddle. Butter the buns and then place them, flat side down, on the griddle and cook until golden brown, about 1½ minutes. Spread a generous tablespoon of the sauce on the top half of each bun.

6. Place a patty on the bottom half of each bun. Mound a heap of caramelized onions on the patty. Add the bun top to each. Transfer each to a dinner plate and serve, with the remaining sauce passed on the side.

The EMMY Double Stack: Divide the burger meat into 8 thin patties. Substitute American cheese for the Cheddar and add sliced bread-and-butter pickles atop the cheese. Cook the burgers for 1½ minutes per side and let stand for about 3 minutes before building the burger.

Grafton Village Cheddar, handmade in Vermont, is sharp and more assertive than other Cheddars you might find in the supermarket. It has a rectangular shape that cuts into perfect slices for topping a beef patty. A wire-style cheese slicer does the job easily at home. If you use another aged Cheddar, try to use slices about 3½ inches (9 cm) square and about ¼ inch (6 mm) thick.

CHAPTER 7

SANDWICHES

Years ago, during his final exam at the Institute of Culinary Education, while all of Matt's classmates were busy creating classic French dishes and employing traditional Italian techniques to show off their learned skills, Matt was hyper-focused on using his skills to execute a perfect sandwich. When the panel of teachers arrived at his station and he presented his culminating dish—a chicken cutlet sandwich—the group was initially confounded; they had to step away to confer. They were used to students using the exam to actualize classics and were baffled that a student would have the audacity to make a sandwich his capstone project. But then, they tasted the sandwich, and they listened as Matt described how he diligently employed key techniques to build the sauce, bread and fry the cutlet, and develop an enriched flavor profile. Tickled, they passed him and lauded his contemporary and practical approach. So here, we offer some staple sandwiches that honor one of Matt's most favorite styles of food.

ROAST BEEF SANDWICH WITH MISO QUESO

MAKES 6 SANDWICHES

When compiling recipes for this book, we reached back to dishes that we had featured as daily menu specials. One person mentioned "that roast beef sandwich with the miso queso," and the entire group gave a collective sigh of approval. Eye of round is a good choice for roast beef sandwiches because it's easy to slice. But don't cook it above medium-rare, or this lean cut will dry out. The Vietnamese fried shallots may remind you of American fried onions, perhaps like the topping on your mom's holiday green bean casserole, but we find this version to be much tastier. Allow at least 18 hours for the beef to marinate in the refrigerator.

MISO-CRUSTED ROAST BEEF
½ cup (140 g) red (*aka*) miso
2 teaspoons Korean chili flakes
2 teaspoons kosher salt
1 teaspoon sugar
1 eye of round beef roast, about 3 pounds (1.4 kg)

1 cup (240 ml) Miso Queso (page 203)
6 sandwich buns, preferably Pretzel Buns (page 210), split
24 slices bread-and-butter pickles, as needed
½ cup (30 g) Vietnamese fried shallots

1. To prepare the roast: Mix the miso, chili flakes, salt, and sugar in a small bowl. Place the beef on a large piece of plastic wrap. Using a silicone or rubber spatula, spread the rub all over the beef (the cure will stick to the wrap). Wrap the roast and slip it into a large resealable plastic bag. Refrigerate for at least 18 or up to 24 hours.

2. Position a rack in the center of the oven and preheat the oven to 450°F (230°C).

3. Unwrap the beef, reserving any cure clinging to the wrap. Place the beef on a roasting rack set in a roasting pan. Spread a tablespoon or two of the reserved miso cure in a thin layer over the top and sides of the beef. Discard the remaining miso cure.

4. Roast for 15 minutes. Reduce the oven temperature to 350°F (180°C). Continue roasting until the miso has formed a dark crust on the beef and an instant-read thermometer inserted in the center of the roast registers 125°F (51°C), about 1 hour. Remove from the oven and let stand for 10 minutes.

5. Heat the miso queso in a small saucepan over low heat, stirring occasionally, until hot and melted, about 3 minutes.

6. Transfer the roast beef to a carving board, preferably one with a well to catch the carving juices. Using a very sharp carving knife, cut the roast crosswise into thin slices. For each sandwich, stack the sliced beef on the bottom half of a roll. (Unless you like overloaded sandwiches, you will have leftover sliced beef—lucky you!) Top with a couple of tablespoons of the miso queso, 4 pickles, and a tablespoon or so of the fried shallots. Dip the top bun half in the carving juices and place it on the bottom half of the sandwich. Cut the sandwich in half and serve.

Miso is essentially ground and fermented soybeans and salt, sometimes mixed with other ingredients like barley or rice. There are three main types, classified by their color, which also corresponds to their depth of flavor. White (*shiso*) miso is made from soybeans and rice, lightly fermented, and mild. Yellow (*shinshu*) miso, created with a mix of soybeans and barley, is a step up in deeper flavor. Red (*aka*) miso, with its longer fermentation and inclusion of darker grains, has the most pungent taste. While mild white miso may be the most versatile of the three, we reach for red miso most often for its full flavor.

RHODE ISLAND CHORIZO SANDWICH WITH KALE AND PROVOLONE

MAKES 4 SANDWICHES

Rhode Island, a home to Portuguese culture, is where we met at Roger Williams University and where Emily learned the ropes of waiting tables at The Casual Inn, a family-run Portuguese restaurant. Spicy sausages, such as chouriço and linguiça, are a big part of the cuisine. This sandwich, similar to a sloppy Joe, is the kind of rib-sticking fare that would revive a fisherman after a long day of pulling in nets on the high seas. Some Portuguese butchers make an unsmoked fresh bulk chouriço, but because it isn't easy to find, you can substitute Mexican-style chorizo, which is very similar and also seasoned with paprika and garlic. Serve these on traditional crusty hero rolls instead of the pretzel buns we use for our other sandwiches.

FILLING

1½ pounds (680 g) bulk Mexican chorizo, casings removed
2 teaspoons whole cumin seeds
1 large green bell pepper, seeded and thinly sliced
1 small red onion, thinly sliced
2 garlic cloves, minced
1 cup (240 ml) canned crushed tomatoes
2 tablespoons hot red pepper sauce, preferably Cholula

4 sesame hero rolls, split and toasted
8 thin slices sharp provolone
4 handfuls baby kale
½ cup (75 g) sliced pickled banana peppers
½ cup (60 g) pitted and coarsely chopped Castelvetrano olives
2 teaspoons celery seeds

1. To make the filling: Cook the chorizo in a large, heavy skillet, preferably cast iron, over medium-high heat, breaking up the meat with the side of a wooden spoon and stirring occasionally, until the sausage is lightly browned and has rendered some of its fat, about 8 minutes. Stir in the cumin. Add the bell pepper, red onion, and garlic and cook, stirring occasionally, until the vegetables soften, about 5 minutes. Stir in the tomatoes, ½ cup (120 ml) water, and the hot sauce and bring to a simmer, scraping up any browned bits in the skillet. Reduce the heat to low and simmer, stirring occasionally, until the sauce thickens and the vegetables are very tender, about 20 minutes.

2. Divide the filling among the rolls and top each with 2 provolone slices and a handful of the kale. Serve with the banana peppers, olives, and celery seeds on the side so each person can add them as they wish.

EMMALETTA

MAKES 6 TO 8 SANDWICHES

A specialty of the Central Grocery near the French Market, the hefty muffaletta overflows with Italian heritage in the form of mortadella, soppressata, and provolone cheese layered in a split loaf of bread slathered with a marinated olive salad. Here's how we make it with three of our favorite pickled foods; Castelvetrano olives, cornichons, and banana peppers. If your cornichons include onions in the jar, substitute them for the vinegar-pickled onions. Be sure to let it rest for a few hours before serving to marry the flavors.

OLIVE SALAD
1 generous tablespoon coarsely chopped yellow onion
2 tablespoons rice wine vinegar
1 generous cup (180 g) Castelvetrano olives, pitted
2 tablespoons coarsely chopped pickled banana peppers
2 tablespoons coarsely chopped cornichons (tiny sour pickles)
2 tablespoons extra-virgin olive oil
Freshly ground black pepper

1 round loaf artisan bread with sesame seed topping, about 1¼ pounds
   (570 g)
½ cup (120 ml) extra-virgin olive oil
8 ounces (225 g) thinly sliced provolone
8 ounces (225 g) thinly sliced mortadella
8 ounces (225 g) thinly sliced soppressata

1. To make the salad: Combine the onion and vinegar in a small ramekin or custard cup. Let stand at room temperature for 1 to 2 hours. Do not drain.

2. Pulse the olives, onion, banana peppers, and cornichons in a food processor until chopped. Add the oil and pulse to combine. Transfer to a bowl. Season to taste with pepper. Cover and refrigerate for at least 1 hour or up to 5 days.

3. Using a serrated knife, split the bread in half lengthwise. Drizzle each cut side with half of the oil. Spread the olive salad on the bottom half. Cover with provolone, mortadella, and soppressata, and finish with the bread top, cut side down. Wrap the muffaletta in plastic wrap. Place on a baking sheet. Top with another baking sheet and weigh the sheet down with four or five heavy cans to press the sandwich. Let stand at room temperature for 1 to 2 hours, or refrigerate the entire setup for up to 8 hours.

4. If refrigerated, let stand at room temperature for 1 hour before serving. Cut into wedges and serve.

LAMMY BURGER WITH ACHAAR SPREAD AND GREEN PAPAYA SALAD

MAKES 4 BURGERS

Once the EMMY Burger was perfected, Matt became excited to explore new burger options. Other burger ideas popped into our heads, and Matt landed upon using lamb meat. The secret sauce has a yogurt base, flavored with Indian mango pickle, called achaar. You will have leftover achaar—all the better for serving on the side of the burger, because you will want more of this wonderful spread. We also put a toasted and folded papadum on the burger for some interesting crunch. Use any kind of papadum you like, as the spiced versions will add another layer of flavor that can be pleasantly surprising.

ACHAAR SPREAD

1 cup (240 ml) cup plain Greek whole-milk or low-fat (but not nonfat) yogurt

3 heaping tablespoons "cut" hot Indian mango pickle, with any clinging sauce, finely chopped

2 tablespoons minced carrot

2 tablespoons finely chopped salted cashews

2 tablespoons unseasoned rice wine vinegar

TOASTED PAPADUMS

4 plain or spiced papadums

GREEN PAPAYA TOPPING

1 cup (100 g) peeled, seeded, and julienned green papaya (about one-quarter papaya), cut on a mandoline or V-slicer

2 tablespoons fresh cilantro leaves

½ teaspoon kosher salt

½ teaspoon sugar

BURGERS

2 pounds (910 g) ground lamb

2 teaspoons kosher salt

1 teaspoon freshly ground black pepper, as needed

4 sandwich buns, preferably Pretzel Buns (page 210), split

1. To make the spread: Mix all of the ingredients in a small bowl. Cover and refrigerate for at least 1 hour or up to 3 days. Remove from the refrigerator 1 hour before using to lose its chill.

2. To prepare the papadums: Heat a large, empty skillet over high heat. One at a time, add a papadum and cook, turning occasionally with a pancake turner or tongs, until the papadum is covered with tiny bubbles but is still flexible, about 1 minute. Transfer to a plate and quickly fold the papadum into quarters before it starts to cool and crisp. Return to the skillet and cook on both sides for another 30 seconds or so to crisp a bit more. Stack each folded papadum on a plate as you go and let it cool completely.

3. To make the green papaya topping: Mix all of the ingredients in a small bowl.

4. To cook the burgers: Heat a large, heavy skillet or griddle (preferably cast iron) over medium-high heat. Shape the lamb into four 4-inch (10-cm) burgers. Season the burgers with the salt. Add to the skillet and cook, turning once or twice, until browned on both sides, 8 minutes total for medium-rare. While cooking, grind the pepper over the burgers. (The pepper will release more of its flavor when it comes in contact with the hot skillet.) Transfer the burgers to a wire rack set on a baking sheet and let stand for 3 minutes. Warm the buns, cut sides down, in batches, in the skillet while the burgers are standing.

5. For each burger, place a portion of meat on the bottom half of a bun. Top with about 2 tablespoons of the spread and one-quarter of the green papaya mixture and a folded papadum. Add the burger top and serve, with additional spread passed on the side.

Mangoes and Green Papayas Mangoes and papayas grow everywhere throughout Asia, and they're so ubiquitous that cooks don't always wait for them to get ripe and sweet for eating.

Achaar is sold jarred in many varieties: sliced, diced, hot, mild, extra hot, in mustard oil, and more. We use Udupi-style cut mango in a spicy sauce, but any kind will work. Even though it's already cut, chop the mango bits even more finely before adding to the yogurt for the burger spread. You'll find mango pickle at all Indian markets and some well-stocked supermarkets.

Green papaya is usually eaten raw as a salad, and the Thai version is particularly well known and delicious. Choose a fruit that is firm and without any blemishes. Skin the fruit with a vegetable peeler, cut it in half lengthwise, and scoop out and discard the black seeds. The papaya is now ready for further cutting.

CRISP AND SPICY CHICKEN SANDWICH

MAKES 4 SANDWICHES

Here's another recipe that proves having your fridge stocked with great condiments and dressings, such as Nguyen Sauce and our Chive Ranch Dressing, helps you pull off your favorite dishes with little effort. With these on hand, a simple chicken sandwich becomes an event. Be sure to allow at least 4 hours to soak the chicken in the buttermilk brine.

CRISPY CHICKEN THIGHS

2 cups buttermilk
½ cup (120 ml) gochujang
1 tablespoon kosher salt
2 teaspoons sugar
4 boneless, skinless chicken thighs, 4 to 5 ounces each
½ cup (60 g) unbleached all-purpose flour
2 large eggs
1 cup (70 g) panko (Japanese bread crumbs)
Vegetable oil, for frying

4 sandwich rolls, preferably Pretzel Buns (page 210), split
4 tablespoons (60 ml) Nguyen Sauce (page 198)
½ cup (120 ml) Chive Ranch Dressing (page 199)
8 cornichons, cut lengthwise into thin slices
2 large radishes, cut lengthwise into thin slices

1. Whisk the buttermilk, gochujang, salt, and sugar in a medium bowl. Trim the chicken of excess fat. Where the chicken is thickest, make a deep horizontal incision and open up the flap to make the thigh as evenly thick as possible. Add the chicken to the buttermilk mixture and turn to coat. Cover and refrigerate, occasionally turning the chicken over, for at least 4 or up to 12 hours.

2. Position racks in the top third and center of the oven and preheat the oven to 200°F (95°C). Line a small rimmed baking sheet (quarter-sheet pan) with a wire rack.

3. Put the flour in a shallow bowl. Beat the eggs until combined in a second bowl. Put the panko in a third bowl. One at a time, remove a chicken thigh from the buttermilk mixture, letting the excess liquid drain into the bowl. Coat the chicken in the flour, then in the eggs, and finally in the panko. Place on the baking sheet.

4. Pour enough oil to come about ½ inch (12 mm) up the sides of a large skillet. Heat over medium-high heat until the oil registers 350°F (180°C) on a deep-frying thermometer.

5. In batches and without crowding, add the chicken and cook, turning once, adjusting the heat as needed so the chicken doesn't brown too quickly, until the crust is golden brown and the chicken is cooked through, about 6 minutes. Transfer the chicken to the rack on the baking sheet and keep warm on the center rack of the oven while cooking the remaining chicken. During the last few minutes, place the opened rolls in the top rack to warm.

6. Using a rubber spatula, spread 1 tablespoon Nguyen sauce on top of each chicken thigh. Spread the ranch dressing over both cut sides of the rolls, as desired. On the bottom half of each roll, place the chicken and top with some of the radishes and the cornichons. Add the roll tops. Cut each sandwich in half and serve immediately.

SMOKED CHICKEN SANDWICH WITH YUZU AÏOLI

MAKES 4 SANDWICHES

Thinking outside of the ketchup-mayo-mustard box, we developed this yuzu sauce specifically as a spread for this sandwich. Chicken thighs are the best choice here, as breast meat tends to dry out, even with careful grilling. While we cook the chicken in the wood oven in our West Village location, it can also be broiled. Start a couple of hours ahead to pickle the cucumbers.

CUCUMBER PICKLES

½ cup (120 ml) rice vinegar

2 tablespoons sake

½ teaspoon sugar

½ teaspoon kosher salt

Pinch of crushed hot red pepper flakes

½ seedless (English) cucumber, thinly sliced into rounds (about 32)

YUZU SAUCE

⅔ cup (165 ml) Aïoli (page 201)

1 tablespoon sweet soy sauce

1½ teaspoons yuzu juice

¼ teaspoon five-spice powder

CHICKEN

6 boneless, skinless chicken thighs, about 4 ounces (115 g) each

Canola oil, as needed

1 teaspoon kosher salt

½ teaspoon five-spice powder

½ teaspoon freshly ground black pepper

4 sandwich rolls, preferably Pretzel Buns (page 210), split

8 thin tomato slices

Special equipment: Large handful of maple or oak chips (or a combination)

1. To make the pickles: Stir the vinegar, sake, sugar, salt, and pepper flakes in a shallow nonreactive glass or ceramic bowl or dish to dissolve the sugar and salt. Add the cucumbers and mix. Let stand at room temperature for 1 to 2 hours. (The pickles can be covered and refrigerated for up to 2 days.) Drain well.

2. To make the sauce: Whisk the aïoli, sweet soy sauce, yuzu juice, and five-spice powder in a small bowl.

3. To prepare the chicken: Brush the chicken with the oil. Mix the salt, five-spice powder, and black pepper in a small bowl. Season the chicken all over with the mixture. Let stand while building the fire.

4. Prepare an outdoor grill for indirect cooking over medium heat (350°F/180°C). For a charcoal fire, let the fire burn until the coals are coated with white ash, then sprinkle the chips over the coals. For a gas grill, add the chips to the smoker box.

5. When the chips are smoking, add the chicken, skinned side down, to the empty area of the grill. Cover the grill and cook, turning once, until the chicken feels firm when pressed on the thickest part with your forefinger (it is difficult to gauge the temperature of this thin cut with an instant-read thermometer), about 45 minutes. Move the chicken, skin side down, to the heated area of the grill and cook to crisp and brown the skin, 1 to 2 minutes. If the fat from the chicken makes flare-ups, move the chicken to the unheated area of the grill. During the last few minutes, toast the rolls on the grill. Remove the chicken and rolls from the grill.

6. Let the chicken cool on a cutting board for about 3 minutes. Using two forks, pull the meat into large shreds. Drain the pickles well. Spread the rolls with the yuzu aïoli. Build each sandwich on a roll with a chicken thigh, about 8 pickled cucumber slices, and 2 tomato slices. Cut in half and serve with any remaining sauce passed on the side.

DUCK CONFIT SANDWICH WITH XIANNAISE

MAKES 4 SANDWICHES

We've had a couple of duck sandwiches on the menu over the years, but this is the one that keeps making return guest appearances. It began life as a pressed-duck sandwich, but the "pulled" approach is easier to accomplish at home. Although the instructions may look complicated, there is actually very little prep involved.

DUCK CONFIT
1½ teaspoons Sichuan peppercorns
¾ teaspoon black peppercorns
1 tablespoon kosher salt
1½ teaspoons sugar
1½ teaspoons Korean red chili flakes
6 duck leg quarters (about 3 lb/1.4 kg)
1 cup (240 ml) rendered duck fat, melted and warm, or extra-virgin
   olive oil

4 sandwich buns, preferably Pretzel Buns (page 210), split
1 Persian cucumber, cut paper thin on a mandoline or V-slicer
1 scallion, white and green parts, cut into thin shreds
4 leaves Bibb lettuce
⅔ cup (165 ml) Xiannaise (page 202), as needed

1. To make the confit: Grind the Sichuan and black peppercorns in an electric spice or coffee grinder. Add the salt, sugar, and chili flakes and pulse to combine.

2. Place the duck on a baking sheet. Season the duck all over with the spice mixture, rubbing it in with your fingers, making sure all of the mixture is clinging to the duck. Place the duck, skin side up, on a wire rack set on a rimmed baking sheet. Refrigerate, uncovered, for at least 18 or up to 24 hours.

3. Position a rack in the center of the oven and preheat the oven to 350ºF (180ºC). Quickly rinse the duck under cold running water and wipe off most of the spice mixture with paper towels—some of it can remain on the skin. Place the duck, skin side down, in a baking dish large enough to hold it snugly. Bake, uncovered, for 30 minutes. Remove the baking dish from the oven. Turn the duck skin side up and pour in the melted duck fat. Cover the baking dish tightly with aluminum foil. Return to the oven. Reduce the oven temperature to 300ºF (150ºC). Continue baking until the meat is very tender, about 1½ hours. Remove from the oven, uncover, and let the duck stand until easy to handle and still warm, about 45 minutes.

4. Transfer the duck to a carving board and reserve the fat in the baking dish. Discard the duck skin, bones, and gristle. Using your fingers, shred the duck into bite-

sized pieces. Transfer the meat to a medium bowl and pour in all the reserved duck fat—it does not have to cover the duck. Let cool. Cover the dish and refrigerate for at least 1 or up to 3 days.

5. When ready to serve, transfer the duck and any clinging fat to a large skillet. Cook over medium heat, stirring often, until the duck is heated through and the fat is melted, about 5 minutes.

6. For each sandwich, use a slotted spoon to heap the duck on the bottom half of the roll. Strain the duck fat and reserve for another use. Top with a few cucumber slices, some scallion shreds, and a lettuce leaf. Generously spread the top half of the bun with about 2 tablespoons of the Xiannaise and close the sandwich. Serve immediately.

Duck fat Here's a simple truth: Duck is delicious. We cook with it a lot, especially when coming up with daily specials for the menu. While the meat itself is dense and tasty, it's the duck fat that is especially prized by cooks for its incredibly rich flavor.

When duck roasts, the fat in and under the skin will render out. When the duck is cooked, strain the fat into a heatproof container to remove any solids, and let it cool. Refrigerate the fat until it is solid. Lift out the block of chilled fat and wipe away any collected juices with a paper towel. Reheat the fat just to melt it and pour into a clean container. The fat can be refrigerated for up to two weeks or frozen for up to three months. Leftover duck fat is fantastic for cooking, especially sautéed potatoes.

LOBSTER SALAD SANDWICH

MAKES 4 SANDWICHES

Our lobster sandwich is prepared with Southeast Asian flavors that truly complement the sweet lobster meat. The herb combo of Thai basil and cilantro is key. It is best to have all of the components prepared and then toss them together at the last minute so the herbs retain their fresh flavor and color.

GARLIC CHIPS
1 large plump garlic clove, peeled without crushing
Vegetable oil, for frying

LOBSTER SALAD
2 tablespoons hot water
1 tablespoon coarsely grated palm sugar or light brown sugar
1 pound cooked lobster meat, cut into bite-sized pieces
2 tablespoons coarsely chopped fresh Thai basil
1 tablespoon coarsely chopped fresh cilantro
3 tablespoons fresh lime juice
1 tablespoon fish sauce
Garlic Chips (see above)

4 sandwich rolls, preferably Pretzel Buns (page 210), split
Softened butter, for the rolls
½ cup (120 ml) Kewpie mayonnaise
4 tablespoons (15 g) Vietnamese fried shallots

1. To make the garlic chips: Using a sharp thin knife, carefully shave the garlic crosswise into paper-thin slices. Pour enough oil to come 1 inch (2.5 cm) up the sides of a small, heavy saucepan and heat over high heat until the oil registers 300ºF (150ºC) on an instant-read thermometer. Put the garlic in a small wire sieve. Dip the bottom of the sieve in the oil to just cover the garlic. Fry, stirring the garlic in the sieve with a fork, until the oil is bubbling and the garlic turns golden brown, 30 seconds to 1 minute. This low-heat method is much more reliable than just tossing the garlic into the hot oil and fishing the slices out, as the last slices out tend to burn. It is also a good idea to do a trial run with a few slices to establish the cooking time. Transfer the garlic to paper towels to drain, crisp, and cool. Discard the garlic-flavored oil or cool it and refrigerate to use in salad dressings or stir fries.

2. To make the salad: Combine the hot water and palm sugar in a small custard cup or ramekin and let stand for 3 minutes to soften the sugar. Heat on high in a microwave oven, stirring occasionally, until the water is boiling; stir well to dissolve the sugar. (Or combine the water and palm sugar in a small saucepan and heat over low heat, stirring constantly, until the syrup is simmering and the sugar is dissolved.) Remove from the heat and let cool completely.

3. Toss the lobster meat, basil, cilantro, lime juice, fish sauce, garlic chips, and palm sugar syrup in a large bowl.

4. Position a broiler rack about 6 inches (15 cm) from the heat source and preheat on Broil/High. Toast the rolls in the broiler. Remove the rolls from the broiler, butter them, and set them aside.

5. Spread the mayonnaise on the rolls. Divide the lobster salad and shallots evenly among the bottom halves of the rolls. Add the roll tops and serve immediately.

Palm sugar is an unrefined sugar made from the boiled sap of various palm trees, most typically the date palm. It is sold in blocks, patties, or cakes and must be chopped before using. Just shave off what you need with a large knife and chop it up. Light brown sugar is an acceptable substitute.

Lobster meat can be purchased from top-quality fishmongers. One pound of lobster meat is the equivalent of about three 1¾-pound (800 g) lobsters.

Fried shallots are a crunchy Vietnamese condiment sold in large jars. We like them on our sandwiches. Look for palm sugar and fried shallots at your local Asian market.

CHAPTER 8

PASTA

We are not an Italian restaurant, but we will sometimes offer pasta dishes as daily specials. Matt's pasta dishes, in particular, serve as a reminder of how the notion of simplicity can enhance a flavor experience as well as how care and attention to a dish like ragù can create layers of flavor. As with our other offerings, it's important to us to serve pasta that's just a bit different from what people might expect. Instead of the typical meat ragù, we prefer to use duck. Our cheesy shells have an array of different cheeses and include tomatoes, too. Both of these take a little time; we also give recipes for weeknight pasta dinners that can be tossed together without a lot of effort. Like so many foods, you only get out of pasta what you put into it. Cheap, inexpensive pasta does not make a memorable meal. For the best results, search out artisanal brands. Our favorite is Sfoglini, made in Brooklyn with high-quality grains.

BUCATINI ALL'AMATRICIANA

MAKES 4 TO 6 SERVINGS

This classic dish from Amatrice of thick pasta coated with pork-infused tomato sauce is Matt's absolutely favorite bowl of pasta. It's one of the easiest and quickest pasta dishes, and we usually cook up the sauce while the pasta water is coming to a boil. Add a dash of Vietnamese fish sauce to lend a bit of extra umami along with a knob of butter for the richness that olive oil just can't provide.

1 tablespoon extra-virgin olive oil, plus more for serving

4 ounces (115 g) guanciale or thick-sliced bacon, cut into ¼-inch (6-mm) dice

¼ cup (30 g) finely chopped red onion

One 28-ounce (784 g) can crushed tomatoes

1 pound bucatini or perciatelli

½ cup (50 g) freshly grated pecorino Romano, plus more for serving

3 tablespoons unsalted butter, at room temperature

½ teaspoon Vietnamese fish sauce, preferably Three Crabs

Kosher salt and freshly ground black pepper

4 to 6 whole basil leaves, for garnishing

1. Add the olive oil and guanciale to a low-heat pan and cook until some of the fat has rendered. Then add the red onion and cook until they are sweated—soft but not brown—about 3 minutes. Stir in the tomatoes and bring to a boil over high heat. Reduce the heat to very low to keep the sauce barely simmering.

2. Meanwhile, bring a large pot of salted water to a boil over high heat. Add the bucatini and cook according to the package directions until al dente. Scoop out and reserve about a cup (120 ml) of the pasta cooking water. Drain the pasta well and return to the pot. Add the tomato sauce, ½ cup (50 g) Romano, butter, and fish sauce. Toss to coat the pasta, adding enough of the reserved water to loosen the sauce. Season to taste with salt and pepper.

3. Transfer to a serving bowl, drizzle with olive oil, and garnish with basil leaves. Serve immediately, with more grated cheese on the side for sprinkling.

Guanciale is an Italian cured meat product. Its fat renders and infuses food with a deep, porky flavor. Pork jowls are rubbed with spices and salt and hung for a few weeks to cure. Thick sliced American bacon can be used as a substitute. You'll easily find guanciale at Italian specialty food stores. Wrapped well in plastic and refrigerated, it keeps for months.

TIPS FOR MAKING PASTA

Don't skimp on the cooking water. For every pound of water, bring at least 3 quarts (2.8 L) water to a boil in a pot over high heat. You really want the pasta to swim in the water.

Always cook pasta in salted water. If the water is unsalted, the pasta will taste very bland. Cooking pasta is not a time to use just a pinch. Use about 2 teaspoons kosher salt per quart, or 2 tablespoons for 3 quarts. The water should be salty as the ocean.

At our restaurants, we usually cook one order of pasta at a time. The pasta is cooked until it is al dente; then it's drained and finished off in a skillet with the sauce, where it will cook further. We have modified the procedure slightly for at-home cooking. The pasta will soak in some of the sauce during this second cooking.

Before draining the pasta, scoop out and reserve about one cup's worth of the cooking water (240 ml). This slightly starchy water will be tossed into the pasta and sauce mixture to help the amalgamation and to lightly dilute thick sauces.

Matt often adds a dash of Vietnamese fish sauce to his pasta sauces to give an extra hint of umami and salinity. This is a useful trick you can try with all your pasta sauces. Don't overdo the fish sauce—it should add just a hint of underlying flavor.

CAMPANELLE WITH DUCK RAGÙ

MAKES 6 SERVINGS

Our duck ragù is a big fan favorite. Matt perfected this dish in our home kitchen for more than a decade before introducing it at our original location in 2014. Of everything Matt makes, his duck ragù is the exemplar of how he cooks with love and care. Some people use the word *ragù* to describe any old Italian pasta sauce, but it really refers to the thick and meaty variety, like this incredibly rich version made with duck, vegetables, and herbs. For the best flavor, make the ragù the day before and refrigerate it overnight so the fat rises to the top. But—and here is the true secret of this dish—don't remove all of the fat; instead, emulsify it into the base. Campanelle, or "bells" in Italian, is our favorite shape for this dish, but our favorite brand, Sfoglini, calls this shape "trumpets." Nonetheless, any sturdy and curly pasta works well to catch the thick ragù in its nooks and crannies.

RAGÙ

1 duck (5 lb/2.3 kg), neck and giblets reserved
4 carrots, finely diced (about 8 oz/225 g)
1 yellow onion, finely chopped (about 8 oz/225 g)
1 cup (225 g) tomato paste
2 cups (240 ml) dry white wine
1 quart (960 ml) duck stock
4 large, leafy sprigs fresh sage
4 large, leafy sprigs fresh thyme
1 large, leafy sprig fresh rosemary
Kosher salt and freshly ground black pepper

1 pound (455 g) campanelle or other tubular pasta
3 tablespoons unsalted butter, at room temperature
1 teaspoon Vietnamese fish sauce, preferably Three Crabs
Whole nutmeg, for grating
Grated pecorino Romano, for serving
Fresh small sage leaves, for garnish

1. To make the ragù: Start at least one day before serving. Cut off the long flap of neck skin where it meets the duck's body and chop it into 2-inch (5-cm) pieces. Using a cleaver, poultry shears, or a large knife, cut the duck into quarters. Chop the neck into 2 or 3 chunks; the neck and giblets should be used for a stock with the duck bones. Remove the breast meat from the bone and grind in a grinder or food processor.

2. Heat a large, heavy saucepan or Dutch oven over medium-high heat. Add the chopped skin and cook, stirring occasionally, until it renders a few tablespoons of fat, about 3 minutes. Add the duck leg quarters, skin side down, and cook until the skin is browned, 7 to 10 minutes. Turn and brown the other side, about 3 minutes. Transfer the duck legs to a plate, leaving the fat in the pan. Repeat to cook the ground duck breast.

3. Add the carrots and onion to the saucepan with the ground duck meat and cook, stirring occasionally, until the vegetables are softened, about 5 minutes. Stir in the tomato paste and cook, stirring occasionally, until it shows a darker red on the bottom of the pan. Using a wooden spoon, stir well to loosen the browned bits in the bottom of the pan, and repeat two or three times to lightly toast the tomato paste for richer flavor and color. Add the wine and stir well to dissolve the tomato paste. Stir in the stock. Tie the sage, thyme, and rosemary into a bundle (bouquet garni) with kitchen twine. Return the duck legs to the pot and add the bouquet garni. Pour in enough duck stock to barely cover the duck.

4. Bring to a boil over high heat. Reduce the heat to low and cover with the lid ajar. Simmer, occasionally turning the duck and stirring the sauce, until the duck is very tender, 1½ to 1¾ hours. Remove from the heat.

5. Using kitchen tongs, transfer the duck legs to a platter and discard the bouquet garni. Let the duck cool until it is easy to handle, about 30 minutes. Discard the duck skin and bones and pick the warm meat with your fingers. Then put the torn leg meat back into the larger mixture. Season to taste with salt and pepper.

6. Let cool. The Ragù is ready to use or can be refrigerated for use at a later time.

7. Bring a large pot of well-salted water to a boil over high heat. Add the pasta and cook according to the package directions until al dente. Drain well and return the pasta to the pot. Add the ragù, butter, and fish sauce. Cook over low heat, stirring occasionally, just until the sauce barely comes to a simmer.

8. Spoon the pasta and its sauce into individual bowls. Using a Microplane or the smallest holes on a box grater, grate a good amount of nutmeg over each serving. Sprinkle with Romano. Top with the sage leaves. Serve immediately.

PASTA WITH ARUGULA AND PISTACHIO PESTO

MAKES 4 TO 6 SERVINGS

While basil is the base of the best-known pestos, here is our version using slightly peppery arugula and the rich taste of pistachios. Blanching helps to brighten the arugula, and pistachio accents the green color. Pistachio oil is the best choice here, but use extra-virgin olive oil as a substitute. You'll have leftover pesto for another use—perhaps experiment with topping a white pizza with your leftover pesto!

PESTO
8 ounces (225 g) baby arugula, about 6 packed cups
¼ cup (30 g) shelled pistachios
¼ cup (25 g) shredded Manchego
2 cloves Garlic Confit (page 207)
Finely grated zest of ¼ large lemon
⅓ cup (75 ml) plus 1 tablespoon pistachio oil
Kosher salt and freshly ground black pepper

1 pound (455 g) spaghetti
½ cup (120 ml) Pesto (see above)
Pistachio oil or extra-virgin olive oil, for drizzling
Grated pecorino Romano, for serving

1. To make the pesto: Bring a large saucepan of water to a boil over high heat. Gradually stir in the arugula and cook just until the leaves turn a darker shade of green, about 1 minute. Drain in a colander. Return the arugula to the saucepan, fill it with cold running water, and let stand until the arugula is cooled, about 1 minute. Drain again. Squeeze the excess liquid from the arugula. You will have only a handful of squeezed-out arugula, so don't be surprised.

2. Pulse the pistachios, Manchego, garlic confit, and lemon zest in a food processor until minced. Add the arugula. Turn the processor on and gradually add the pistachio oil through the feed tube. Season to taste with salt and pepper. Transfer the pesto to a lidded container and press a piece of plastic wrap directly on the surface. Cover with the lid and refrigerate for up to 1 day. Stir well before using.

3. Bring a large pot of well-salted water to a boil over high heat. Add the pasta and cook according to the package directions until al dente. Scoop out and reserve about 1 cup (240 ml) of the pasta cooking water. Drain the pasta and return it to the cooking pot. Add ½ cup (120 ml) of the pesto and toss, adding enough of the reserved cooking water to make a light, clinging sauce. Season the pasta with salt and pepper. (The remaining pesto can be frozen, covered with both plastic wrap directly on the surface and a lid, for up to 1 month. Thaw overnight in the refrigerator before using.)

4. Transfer the pasta to a serving bowl. Serve, drizzling each serving with oil and with more Romano passed on the side.

REGINETTI WITH PEAS, PEA SHOOTS, AND ROMANO

MAKES 4 TO 6 SERVINGS

This simple vegetarian pasta celebrates spring with fresh peas in two incarnations. When cooking with such a small list of ingredients, it's especially important that the components are fresh and high quality. We love to use pea shoots for added texture. In this recipe, the heat only slightly wilts the leaves so you get a bit of fresh crunch in each bite. Reginetti, or "little queen" in Italian, is twisty pasta with curly edges, but any twisty pasta, like radiatore or short fusilli, will do.

> 1 pound (455 g) Reginetti, campanelle, or other short and curly pasta
> 2 tablespoons unsalted butter
> 1 cup (140 g) freshly shelled peas or thawed frozen baby peas
> ½ cup (50 g) freshly grated pecorino Romano, plus more for serving
> Kosher salt and freshly ground black pepper
> 6 ounces (170 g) packed fresh pea shoots, tough hollow stems
>   discarded (about 4 packed cups)
> Extra-virgin olive oil, for serving

1. Bring a large pot of well-salted water to a boil over high heat. Add the pasta and cook according to the package directions until al dente.

2. While the pasta is cooking, melt the butter in a large skillet over medium heat. Add the peas and cover. Cook, stirring occasionally, until they are barely tender, about 5 minutes. (If using thawed frozen peas, just cook them until hot, about 2 minutes.) Set the peas aside in the skillet.

3. Scoop out and reserve about ½ cup (120 ml) of the pasta cooking water. Drain the pasta well. Return the pasta to the cooking pot and add the peas. Sprinkle in the ½ cup (50 g) Romano and toss, adding enough of the water to make a light sauce. Season to taste with salt and pepper.

4. Spoon the pasta into individual pasta bowls and top each with a generous handful of pea shoots. Drizzle with olive oil and serve immediately, with more Romano passed on the side.

Pea shoots are the tender and beautiful ends of the pea vines. They are at their best during late spring and early summer, and can be found at your local greenmarket. Identify them by their fairly large, dark green leaves with a few tendrils peeking through the hollow vines. Those vines can be tough, so it is sometimes necessary to sort through the greens and pick off the ones that are too thick.

CAVATELLI WITH FRESH RICOTTA, LEMON, AND POPPY SEEDS

MAKES 4 TO 6 SERVINGS

This recipe is meant to highlight the high quality of homemade, fresh ricotta, so take advantage of the recipe for this cheese. The combination of lemon zest, poppy seeds, and Romano melds with the ricotta to create a rich, citrusy pasta dish. Cavatelli are tiny discs of eggless semolina pasta, folded over to create the "little hollows" that give it its name. When composing this dish, be sure to bring the ricotta to room temperature before mixing so the cheese doesn't cool down the pasta.

1 pound (455 g) cavatelli, orrechiette, or fusilli
2 cups (480 g) Fresh Ricotta (page 208) at room temperature
½ cup (50 g) freshly grated pecorino Romano, plus more for serving
2 tablespoons poppy seeds
Kosher salt and freshly ground black pepper
1 large lemon, for zesting

1. Bring a large pot of well-salted water to a boil over high heat. Add the pasta and cook according to the package directions until al dente.

2. Scoop out and reserve about ½ cup (120 ml) of the pasta cooking water. Drain the pasta well. Return the pasta to the cooking pot. Add the ricotta and the ½ cup (50 g) Romano and toss, adding enough of the reserved cooking water to make a light, clinging sauce. Sprinkle in the poppy seeds and toss again. Season the pasta with salt and pepper.

3. Transfer the pasta to a serving bowl. Using a Microplane, grate the lemon zest over the top of the pasta. Toss at the table and serve immediately with more Romano passed on the side.

BAKED PINK PASTA WITH FIVE CHEESES

MAKES 6 SERVINGS

This dish is a tribute to Al Forno, in Rhode Island, where we went on our first date, and ate the amazing "Pasta in the Pink." We love the blend of cheese and tomatoes for a rich, pink sauce. For lots of browned, chewy, and irresistible pasta tops, spread the mixture out in a wide skillet or baking dish instead of a deep casserole. Here's a tip you can use any time you make mac 'n' cheese: Undercook the pasta slightly, just until it is barely al dente, as it will soften more during baking.

1 pound (455 g) small pasta shells
2 tablespoons extra-virgin olive oil
1 cup (100 g) shredded fontina, preferably Val d'Aosta
1 cup (100 g) diced (½-inch/12-mm pieces) fresh mozzarella
¾ cup (170 g) Fresh Ricotta (page 208)
¾ cup (75 g) freshly grated pecorino Romano
¾ cup (75 g) crumbled blue cheese
1 cup (240 ml) canned crushed tomatoes
1 cup (240 ml) whole milk
1 tablespoon finely chopped fresh rosemary
Kosher salt and freshly ground black pepper
1 large scallion, white and green parts, thinly sliced on the diagonal

1. Bring a large pot of well-salted water to a boil over high heat. Add the pasta and cook according to the package directions until barely al dente. Drain, rinse under cold running water, and drain well. Toss with the oil.

2. Position a rack in the center of the oven and preheat the oven to 500ºF (260ºC).

3. Mix the fontina, mozzarella, ricotta, Romano, and blue cheese in a large bowl. Transfer half of the mixture to a bowl and reserve. Add the tomatoes, milk, and rosemary and mix well. Add the pasta and mix again to coat. Season to taste with salt and pepper. Spread evenly in a 10-inch (25-cm) cast-iron skillet or a large baking dish. Crumble the reserved cheese mixture on top.

4. Bake until the pasta is bubbling and the top is golden brown, 10 to 15 minutes. Sprinkle with the scallion and serve hot.

CHAPTER 9

DESSERTS

We realize that after one of our pizzas or a big EMMY burger, our guests just might not have room for dessert. Therefore, our dessert menu has to be very tempting in order to entice people to relax their resolve, and their belts, and indulge. Emily, in particular, is a big fan of homey desserts, and we've put many of her childhood favorites on the menu, including blondies, brownies, cheesecake, and cupcakes. Matt goes for more contemporary desserts, such as our corn custard with berries, and "floating islands" flavored with green matcha tea and served in coconut custard sauce. We even have a dessert "pizza" in the form of churros: strips of dough fried and coated with sugar and cinnamon. No matter what you choose, we have worked long and hard to create desserts that we have found to be guaranteed crowd-pleasers. They will be as beloved in your home as they are at the restaurants. It doesn't matter if it is an old-fashioned treat or cutting edge—these sweets are worth the calories.

APPLE CRUMBLE WITH GJETOST CHEESE

MAKES 6 SERVINGS

Apples are *the* fall fruit in New York, so when autumn rolls around, we're sure to add our favorites to the dessert menu. This classic crumble looks traditional at first glance, but we've made some improvements on the classic. While some people like Cheddar cheese with their apple desserts, we love the unusual topping of grated gjetost and a dollop of crème fraîche. We discovered this unique cheese on a visit to the stellar restaurant Please in Cincinnati and could not wait to incorporate it into a dish of our own. We also use this cheese to make a special pizza once in a while, so you might explore and play with this ingredient for your pizzas as well. If gjetost is not readily available, it can be substituted with a sharp cheddar.

CRUMBLE TOPPING
2 cups (260 g) unbleached all-purpose flour
⅔ cup (130 g) packed light brown sugar
⅔ cup plus 1 tablespoon (185 g) unsalted butter, cut into tablespoons, at room temperature
½ teaspoon kosher salt

APPLE FILLING
8 tablespoons (115 g) unsalted butter
5 pounds (2.3 kg) firm apples for baking, peeled, cored, and cut into ½-inch (12-mm) wedges
⅔ cup (130 g) granulated sugar
⅔ cup (130 g) packed light brown sugar
2 tablespoons unbleached all-purpose flour
1½ teaspoons ground cinnamon
½ teaspoon kosher salt
2 teaspoons vanilla extract

One 8.8-ounce (250-g) block gjetost, for grating
Crème fraîche, for serving

1. To make the topping: Pulse the flour, brown sugar, butter, and salt in a food processor (or use your fingertips to work the ingredients together in a bowl) until the mixture is combined and resembles coarse meal. If using a processor, transfer the topping to a large bowl. Press the mixture together into a crumbly mass. (The topping can be covered and stored at room temperature for up to 4 hours.)

2. To make the filling: Melt 4 tablespoons (55 g) of the butter in a 12-inch (30.5-cm) heavy skillet, preferably cast iron, over medium-high heat. When the foam subsides, add half of the apples and cook, turning occasionally, until crisp-tender with some lightly browned slices, 3 to 5 minutes. Do not overcook. Transfer to a large bowl. Repeat with the remaining butter and apples. Return all of the apples to the skillet. Mix in the granulated and brown sugars, flour, cinnamon, and salt and bring to a simmer. Remove from the heat and stir in the vanilla. (The filling can be kept at room temperature for up to 2 hours. Reheat just until beginning to simmer before baking.)

3. Position a rack in the top third of the oven and preheat the oven to 400ºF (200ºC). Crumble the topping all over the filling. Bake until the juices are bubbling and the topping is golden brown, 15 to 20 minutes.

4. Let the crumble cool slightly. Spoon into individual bowls, with the topping facing up. Finely grate the cheese over each serving (as much as you like, but a tablespoon or two will do), and top with a dollop of crème fraîche. Serve immediately.

Apples There are so many apple varieties that choosing the right one for a crumble, pie, or crisp can seem daunting. If you prefer firm apples that hold their shape during baking, choose from Empire, Gala, and eastern-crop Golden Delicious. Many bakers shy away from McIntosh and other varieties that don't stay firm and bake into applesauce, but actually, a couple of these apples combined with solid ones can be nice. If you are shopping at a farmer's market, be sure to ask the vendors for their recommendations for local apples that you might otherwise miss.

Gjetost cheese There simply is no other cheese like Norwegian gjetost, which resembles a big square of caramel candy. The brown color occurs when goat's milk is slowly heated until the natural sugars are caramelized. It is incredibly rich and flavorful, and gjetost is a more esoteric option to enliven a dish.

ANGIE'S CHEESECAKE

MAKES 9 SERVINGS

We have Matt's mom, Angie, to thank for one of our very favorite desserts, this creamy, tangy cheesecake with the iconic New York flavors of sour cream and a hint of lemon. She has been making this cheescake forever and loves to serve it at the end of a Sunday dinner or holiday gathering. If you wish, top it with seasonal fresh fruit—berries, peaches, and cherries are all good—or use the mango purée (page 176) or blueberry sauce (page 178). A tip: Be sure that filling ingredients are at room temperature so they will mix smoothly without any lumps, because overbeating will make the filling rise during baking, then fall and crack when cooled.

CRUST
½ cup (115 g) unsalted butter, melted
1½ cups (140 g) finely crushed graham crackers (from 9 large crackers)

FILLING
2 pounds (910 g) cream cheese, softened
2 cups (400 g) sugar
6 large eggs, lightly beaten, at room temperature
⅓ cup (75 ml) fresh lemon juice
2 tablespoons vanilla extract
1 teaspoon kosher salt
2 pounds (910 g) sour cream, at room temperature

1. To make the crust: Position a rack in the center of the oven and preheat the oven to 350ºF (180ºC).

2. Lightly brush the inside of a 9 x 13-inch (23 x 33-cm) metal baking pan with a little of the melted butter. Stir the cracker crumbs and remaining butter in a medium bowl until evenly moistened. Press the mixture firmly and evenly into the bottom of the pan.

3. Bake until the crust looks set and smells toasty, about 10 minutes. Remove from the oven. Increase the oven temperature to 400ºF (200ºC).

4. To make the filling: Beat the cream cheese and sugar in a large bowl with an electric mixer on medium speed just until smooth. Gradually beat in the eggs. Mix in the lemon juice, vanilla, and salt. If using a standing mixer, remove the bowl from the stand. Add the sour cream and fold it into the filling with a rubber spatula. Spread the filling evenly in the hot crust.

5. Put the baking dish in a large roasting pan. Pour in enough hot water to come about ¾ inch (2 cm) up the sides of the baking dish. Carefully slide the roasting pan onto the oven rack. Bake until sides of the cheesecake have risen a bit, 30 to 40 minutes. Turn the oven off and let the cheesecake rest in the oven about 45 minutes more. Remove from the oven.

6. Lift the cheesecake dish out of the water, transfer to a wire rack, and let cool completely. Cover the pan with plastic wrap. Refrigerate until chilled, at least 3 hours or up to 2 days.

7. Using a sharp thin knife dipped into a tall glass of hot water and dried between cuts, slice and serve chilled. We like to serve in squares!

BUTTERMILK CUPCAKES WITH BOOZY BUTTERCREAM

MAKES 12 CUPCAKES

Cupcakes are popular because they bring back some of the best of our collective childhood memories. This recipe is an adult riff that merges the moist, tender cake with a thick, boozy buttercream.

BUTTERMILK CUPCAKES

1½ cups (195 g) cake flour (not self-rising)
½ teaspoon baking powder
¼ teaspoon baking soda
¼ teaspoon salt
½ cup (115 g) unsalted butter, at room temperature
1 cup (200 g) granulated sugar
2 large eggs, separated, at room temperature
1 teaspoon vanilla extract
½ cup (120 ml) buttermilk, at room temperature

BOOZY BUTTERCREAM

1½ cups (335 g) unsalted butter
3½ cups (250 g) confectioners' sugar, sifted
3 teaspoons bourbon
Pinch of salt
Rainbow sprinkles, for decoration

Special equipment: Pastry bag; ½-inch (12-mm) plain star tip, such as Ateco 865

1. Position a rack in the center of the oven and preheat to 350ºF (180ºC).

2. To make the cupcakes: Sift the flour, baking powder, baking soda, and salt together. Beat the butter in a medium bowl with an electric mixer on high speed until smooth, about 1 minute. Add the sugar and beat until the mixture is light in color and texture, about 3 minutes. One at a time, beat in the yolks, followed by the vanilla. Reduce the mixer speed to low. In thirds, add the flour mixture, alternating with buttermilk, mixing after each addition just until combined. In a separate bowl, using clean beaters, beat the whites with the mixer on high speed just until soft peaks form. Stir about one-third of the whites into the batter to loosen it, and fold in the remaining whites. Divide the batter equally among the cups, filling them only three-quarters full.

3. Bake until the cupcakes are golden brown and spring back when touched lightly on top, 20 to 25 minutes. Let cool for 5 minutes in the cups. Transfer the cupcakes to a wire rack and let cool completely.

4. To make the buttercream: Cut the butter into tablespoons and let it stand at room temperature until slightly softened and pliable but not soft and shiny, about 15 minutes. Cream the butter in a stand mixer on medium speed, add the confectioners' sugar, ½ cup at a time, until smooth. Add in the bourbon, and a touch of salt, and continue on medium until incorporated. This will produce an intentionally thick buttercream. If the frosting is too thick, you can thin it and make it boozier with some added bourbon.

5. Transfer the buttercream to a large pastry bag fitted with a ½-inch (12-mm) plain star tip, such as Ateco 865. Pipe a large swirl of the buttercream over the top of each cupcake. As an option, you can just use an offset spatula to spread the buttercream on the cupcakes. Scatter the sprinkles on the buttercream. The cupcakes are best served the day they are made.

RONA'S BLONDIES WITH CHOCOLATE CHUNKS

MAKES 8 TO 12 BLONDIES

This is another family recipe that was such a part of our lives it just had to be on the EMILY menu. Many years ago, Rona, Emily's mom, stumbled upon a version of this recipe in a newspaper, and has made her adaptation of it ever since. We have nothing against chocolatey brownies, but these chewy, vanilla-y blondies give them a solid run for their money. Although the batter is light-colored, there is a generous amount of chocolate in every bite. Using your favorite bittersweet chocolate instead of chocolate chips is as an easy way to upgrade this old-fashioned favorite.

Softened butter and flour, for the pan
1¾ cups (230 g) unbleached all-purpose flour
1½ teaspoons baking powder
½ teaspoon kosher salt
½ cup (115 g) unsalted butter, at room temperature
¾ cup (150 g) granulated sugar
¾ cup packed (150 g) light brown sugar
3 large eggs, at room temperature
1½ teaspoons vanilla extract
6 ounces (170 g) bittersweet or semisweet chocolate, cut into chunks

1. Position a rack in the center of the oven and preheat the oven to 350ºF (180ºC). Butter the inside of a 9 x 13 x 1-inch (23 x 33 x 2.5-cm) small rimmed baking sheet (quarter-sheet pan). This kind of pan is the perfect size for the blondies and lets you remove them without "digging," but a standard baking pan with 2-inch/5-cm sides will also work. Dust the inside of the pan with flour and tap out the excess flour.

2. Sift the flour, baking powder, and salt through a wire sieve. Beat the butter in a medium bowl with an electric mixer on medium-high speed until creamy, about 1 minute. Gradually beat in the granulated and brown sugars and continue beating until the mixture is light in color and texture, about 3 minutes. One at a time, beat in the eggs, followed by the vanilla. Reduce the mixer speed to low. Add the flour mixture and mix just until combined. Add the chocolate and mix briefly. Spread the batter evenly in the pan.

3. Bake until the top is golden brown and a wooden toothpick inserted in the center comes out clean, about 25 minutes. Transfer to a wire rack. Let cool completely in the pan. Run a knife around the inside of the pan to release the blondies from the edges of the pan. Cut into bars and serve. The blondies can be stored in an airtight container at room temperature for up 3 days.

ROCKY ROAD BROWNIES WITH RUM GANACHE DIP

MAKES 12 BROWNIES

Brownies are on just about everyone's list of favorite desserts, so how do you make them even better? In our opinion, this is accomplished with the "rocky road" addition of marshmallows and walnuts, and by serving the bars with a heady rum-scented dip. Use chocolate chips for the brownie topping because they're softer than bar chocolate and make the bars easier to cut.

BROWNIES

Softened butter, for the pan
½ cup (115 g) unsalted butter, cut into tablespoons
6 ounces (170 g) semisweet or bittersweet chocolate (about 60 percent cacao), finely chopped
½ cup (100 g) packed light brown sugar
2 large eggs, at room temperature
1 teaspoon vanilla extract
1 cup (130 g) unbleached all-purpose flour
¼ teaspoon baking soda
¼ teaspoon salt
1 cup (100 g) coarsely chopped walnuts
½ cup (85 g) semisweet chocolate chips
1½ cups (75 g) miniature marshmallows

GANACHE DIP

½ cup (120 ml) plus about 2 teaspoons heavy cream
6 ounces (170g) bittersweet or semisweet chocolate (about 60 percent cacao), finely chopped
2 tablespoons dark rum, such as Myers's, or additional cream

1. To make the brownies: Position a rack in the center of the oven and preheat the oven to 350ºF (180ºC). Butter an 8-inch (20-cm) square nonstick baking pan.

2. Melt the butter in a medium saucepan over medium heat. Remove from the heat, add the chopped chocolate, and let stand until it softens, 2 to 3 minutes. Whisk until the chocolate is melted and the mixture is smooth. Add the brown sugar and whisk well. One at a time, whisk in the eggs, followed by the vanilla. Sift the flour, baking soda, and salt together. Add to the chocolate mixture and stir until smooth. Stir in half of the walnuts. Scrape the batter into the prepared pan and smooth the top.

3. Bake until a wooden toothpick inserted in the center of the pastry comes out with a few clinging crumbs, about 25 minutes. Transfer to a wire rack. Sprinkle the

chocolate chips evenly over the top and let them stand for about 1 minute to melt slightly. Sprinkle the marshmallows over the chips and spread them out so they come into contact with the chips. The chips will adhere the marshmallows to the top of the brownie. Sprinkle the remaining walnuts over the top of the brownie, again being sure they also come into contact with the melted chips. Gently pat the marshmallows and nuts to be sure they are staying in place. Let cool completely in the pan.

4. Run a small sharp knife around the inside of the pan to pull the brownie away from the edges. Cut into 12 equal bars.

5. When ready to serve, make the ganache dip: Heat the ½ cup (120 ml) cream in a small saucepan until simmering. Remove from the heat. Add the chocolate and let stand until it softens, 2 to 3 minutes. Add the rum and whisk until smooth. Pour the warm ganache into 4 to 6 individual ramekins. Drizzle the 2 teaspoons cream over the top of each as a garnish. Serve the brownies with the ganache for dipping.

PIZZA CHURROS WITH CINNAMON SUGAR

MAKES 12 CHURROS; 4 TO 6 SERVINGS

One of the most popular desserts at EMILY is a pile of freshly fried pizza churros. They are sweet and chewy, like fresh cinnamon-sugar doughnuts. They're just as good at breakfast, served with hot coffee or tea. This is a great way to use up leftover dough if you happen to have some extra after making pizza for last night's dinner.

> 1 ball Round Pie Dough (Mixer or No-Knead, page 68 or 69)
> Vegetable oil, for deep-frying
> ½ cup (100 g) granulated sugar
> ½ teaspoon ground cinnamon

1. Let the dough stand at room temperature for 30 to 45 minutes to lose its chill.

2. Position a rack in the center of the oven and preheat the oven to 350ºF (180ºC). Line a large rimmed baking sheet (half-sheet pan) with a rectangular wire rack. Pour enough oil into a large, heavy saucepan to come about halfway up the sides. Heat over high heat until the oil registers 350ºF (180ºC) on a deep-frying thermometer.

3. On a lightly floured work surface, pat and roll out the dough into a 9 x 6-inch (23 x 15-cm) rectangle. Using a pizza wheel or sharp knife, cut the dough lengthwise into 1-inch (2.5-cm) strips, and cut these vertically in half to make 12 pieces. In batches and without crowding, add the strips to the oil and fry, turning occasionally, until golden brown, about 3 minutes. Using a wire spider or a slotted spoon, transfer the churros to the rack and keep them warm in the oven while frying the remaining strips.

4. Whisk the sugar and cinnamon together in a shallow baking dish. Add the warm churros and toss to coat with the sugar mixture. Stack on a plate and serve warm.

BANANA CREAM PUDDING

MAKES 10 TO 12 SERVINGS

We have long been fans of Greenwich Village's famous Magnolia Bakery, and we admit that we're slightly addicted to their banana pudding. Their recipe is based on a classic version served by many a Southern cook. It is super-simple and unashamedly calls for instant vanilla pudding and a can of condensed milk. This makes a lot of servings, so save it for a big party or plan on sharing it with friends and neighbors. We prefer to serve this dessert parfait-style in Mason jars, as we do at EMILY. If you don't have a dozen jars on hand, get creative and use any tall glassware in the cabinet!

1 can (14 oz/396 g) sweetened condensed milk
1½ cups (360 ml) water
1 box (3.4-oz/96 g) instant vanilla pudding and pie filling
2 cups (480 ml) heavy cream
1 vanilla bean, split lengthwise
2½ cups (210 g) finely crumbled (but not crushed into a powder) vanilla wafers
3 to 4 large bananas, thinly sliced

1. To make the pudding: Whisk the condensed milk and water in a large bowl. Add the pudding mix and whisk for about 2 minutes to thoroughly dissolve the mix. Let stand to thicken, 5 to 10 minutes.

2. Whip the heavy cream in a chilled large bowl with an electric mixer at high speed just until firm peaks form; do not overwhip. Add to the pudding mixture and fold it in with a rubber spatula. Using the tip of a small knife, scrape out the insides of the vanilla bean into the pudding blend. Lightly stir to incorporate.

3. Build the parfaits: Line up your glassware on the counter and then fill the bottom of each jar with about a ¼ inch of crumbled wafers. Next, top with 3 pieces of thinly sliced banana. After that, using a pastry bag, pipe the banana cream pudding into each jar until just below the halfway point. Repeat the process of wafers, bananas, and pudding until the jar is full just below the mouth. Finally top the creation with a final layer of crumbled wafers. If you prefer to serve this dish family-style, simply build your layers in one large, deep bowl. Serve chilled.

Vanilla Pudding and Pie Filling There are many options for instant vanilla pudding and pie filling mix. It's easy to grab the wrong box off the grocery shelf, so here's some advice to help you buy the right kind. Purchase the standard small box with "four ½-cup servings" listed on the front of the package. The most common brand (Jell-O) weighs 3.4 ounces (96 g), contains instant milk in the mix, and uses water. However, the four-serving box of Royal brand weighs 1.85 ounces (52.5 g) and calls for whole milk as the liquid. You can certainly swap them, but use the liquid called for in the directions on the box. Don't buy the larger 5.1-ounce (144-g) box for this recipe. Also, be sure to get instant pudding, not "cook 'n' serve" or "sugar-free."

PISTACHIO SEMIFREDDO WITH RED COMPOTE

MAKES 8 SERVINGS

One of Italy's truly great contributions to the dessert lexicon, semifreddo is a soft ice cream that doesn't require a machine to make. If you can whip egg whites and cream, you can make this frozen beauty. Here is a terrific version with the buttery flavor and the subtle pale green color of pistachios. A juicy compote of strawberries and raspberries contributes a nice tartness to play off the semifreddo's creamy qualities and sets each serving off with a red "sauce." Red currants, if you find them at the farmer's market in the summer, are a fine addition, but totally optional.

SEMIFREDDO
8 large egg whites, at room temperature
1⅔ cups (320 g) granulated sugar
1⅔ cups (400 ml) heavy cream
¾ cup (100 g) finely chopped pistachios

RED COMPOTE
2 cups (400 g) sliced fresh strawberries
1⅓ cups (170 g) fresh raspberries
⅓ cup (60 g) stemmed fresh red currants (optional)
2 tablespoons granulated sugar
2 tablespoons Chambord, framboise, or light rum

2 tablespoons very finely chopped pistachios, for sprinkling

1. To make the semifreddo: Beat the egg whites in a large bowl with an electric mixer on high speed until they begin to form soft peaks. Gradually beat in the sugar and continue beating until stiff, shiny peaks form.

2. Whip the heavy cream in a chilled large bowl with the electric mixer until soft peaks form. Stir about one-quarter of the meringue into the whipped cream to lighten the mixture. Add the remaining meringue with the pistachios and fold together with a rubber spatula until thoroughly combined, keeping the mixture as light as possible.

3. Line a 9 x 5 x 3-inch (23 x 12 x 7.5-cm) loaf pan with a large sheet of plastic wrap, letting the excess plastic hang over the sides. Spread the semifreddo into the pan and bring up the sides of the plastic wrap to cover the top. Freeze for at least 8 hours or up to 2 days.

4. To make the compote: Combine all of the ingredients in a medium bowl. Cover and refrigerate for at least 4 hours. (The compote can be refrigerated for up to 12 hours.)

5. To serve, fold back the plastic wrap to uncover the top of the semifreddo. Invert and unmold the semifreddo onto a chilled serving platter and discard the plastic. Cut into thick slices and transfer to dessert plates. Add the compote with its juices to each serving, sprinkle with pistachios, and serve immediately.

FRUITING ISLANDS OF GREEN TEA MERINGUES AND MANGO PURÉE

MAKES 6 SERVINGS

This dessert has long been a mandatory item on Matt's menus, and it's his favorite way to end a meal. Our take on the French dessert *îles flotantes*, or "floating islands," sports crisp green tea meringues in a pool of creamy coconut sauce and bright orange mango purée. Allow plenty of time for the meringues to slowly cook in a very low oven. Piping them out with a pastry bag gives the best-looking results, but you can simply spoon the meringue into mounds, if you prefer. Of course, you can substitute other fruit purées, such as papaya or berry, for the mango. Once all of the components are ready, the final plating comes together easily, so keep this dessert in mind when you want a stunning finale for your dinner party.

GREEN TEA MERINGUES

4 large egg whites, at room temperature

¾ cup plus 2 tablespoons (175 g) granulated sugar

3½ teaspoons (7 g) matcha (green tea powder)

COCONUT CRÈME ANGLAISE

1 can (13½ oz/385 g) coconut milk, well shaken

5 large egg yolks

¼ cup (50 g) granulated sugar

MANGO PURÉE

2 large ripe mangoes, peeled, pitted, and coarsely chopped

2 tablespoons granulated sugar

1 tablespoon fresh lime juice

Special equipment: Large pastry bag; ½-in (12-mm) star pastry tip, such as Ateco 826

1. To make the meringues: Position a rack in the center of the oven and preheat the oven to 200ºF (95ºC). Line a large rimmed baking sheet (half-sheet pan) with parchment paper.

2. Whip the whites in a large grease-free bowl with an electric mixer on high speed until foamy. A tablespoon at a time, beat in the sugar and continue whipping until the meringue forms stiff, shiny peaks. Sprinkle in the matcha and fold it into the meringue with a rubber spatula. Fit a large pastry bag with a ½-inch-wide (12-mm) star pastry tip, such as Ateco 826. Transfer the meringue to the bag. Pipe 6 large swirls of the meringue onto the prepared sheet pan, spacing them at least 1 inch (2.5 cm) apart.

3. Bake until the meringues are dry and one can be easily picked up and released from the parchment paper, about 2 hours. (If the meringue sticks, continue baking until it releases.) Turn off the oven, prop the oven door ajar with a wooden spoon, and let the meringues cool completely in the oven, about 2 hours more, or preferably overnight. (The cooled meringues can be stored in an airtight container at room temperature for 2 days.)

4. To make the crème anglaise: Heat the coconut milk in a medium, heavy saucepan over medium heat until steaming. Beat the yolks and sugar together in a medium bowl until pale yellow. Gradually beat in the hot coconut milk. Return to the saucepan and reduce the heat to medium-low. Stirring constantly with a wooden spoon, cook until the custard is steaming and thick enough to coat a spoon and leave a trail when you run a finger through it. An instant-read thermometer inserted into the sauce will register about 185°F/85°C. Do not boil. Strain the custard through a wire sieve into a medium bowl. Cover with plastic wrap pressed directly on the surface and pierce a few slits in the wrap to allow the steam to escape. Let cool to room temperature. Refrigerate until chilled, at least 2 hours or up to 2 days.

5. To make the purée: Process the mango, sugar, and lime juice in a blender until smooth. (The purée can be covered and refrigerated for up to 3 days.)

6. To serve, divide the custard among 6 shallow bowls. Add a meringue to each and garnish with dots of the mango purée. Serve immediately.

CORN CUSTARD WITH BLUEBERRIES AND CORN GRANOLA

MAKES 6 SERVINGS

When summer is in full swing, we serve this comforting pudding that showcases two of the season's most iconic ingredients, corn and blueberries. We take freshly fried poha flakes and bake them with a spicy coating to add crunch to the smooth custard and blueberry sauce.

CORN CUSTARD
2 small ears corn
2½ cups (600 ml) heavy cream
1 vanilla bean, split lengthwise
8 large egg yolks
⅓ cup (70 g) granulated sugar

BLUEBERRY SAUCE
2 containers (6 oz/170 g *each*) fresh blueberries (about 2⅔ cups total)
¼ cup (50 g) granulated sugar
2 teaspoons fresh lemon juice

CORN GRANOLA
Canola oil, for deep-frying
2 heaping cups (100 g) corn (also labeled maize) poha
1 large egg white
2 tablespoons light brown sugar
½ teaspoon ground allspice
½ teaspoon ground cinnamon
½ teaspoon freshly grated nutmeg

1 container (6 oz/170 g) fresh blueberries (about 1⅓ cups)

1. To make the corn custard: One at a time, stand a corn ear on its wide end. Using a large knife, cut from top to bottom to slice off the kernels where they meet the cob. Measure the kernels; you should have about 1 cup (180 g). Using the knife blade, scrape the corncobs from the bottom to the top into a medium saucepan to extract the "milk" and add it to the kernels. Chop the cobs crosswise into 2-inch (5-cm) chunks. Put the corncobs, kernels with their milk, cream, and vanilla bean in the saucepan. Bring just to a simmer over medium heat, stirring occasionally. Reduce the heat to very low and infuse the mixture for 30 minutes.

2. Strain the mixture through a fine-mesh wire sieve set over a medium bowl. Discard the corncob pieces. Using a small knife, scrape the vanilla seeds from the pod into the cream, discard the bean, and let the mixture cool to lukewarm. In batches, with the lid ajar to allow any steam to escape, process the corn mixture in a blender (preferably a heavy-duty blender, such as Vitamix), until very smooth.

3. Whisk the yolks and sugar in a medium bowl until pale yellow. Gradually whisk in the corn mixture. Return to the saucepan and cook, stirring constantly with a wooden spoon until the custard is thick enough to coat the spoon and leave a trace when you run a finger through it (185ºF/85ºC on an instant-read thermometer). Strain the custard through the wire sieve into a clean bowl, stirring with a wooden spoon to help the custard flow, and discard any pulp in the sieve. Place the bowl in a larger bowl of ice water and let stand, stirring often, until cool. Cover and refrigerate until well chilled, at least 2 hours or up to 2 days. The custard will be quite thick.

4. To make the blueberry sauce: Cook the blueberries, sugar, and lemon juice in a medium saucepan over medium heat, stirring occasionally, until the berries give off their juices, about 5 minutes. Reduce the heat to low and simmer, stirring often, until the juices thicken slightly and the berries are soft, about 5 minutes more. Remove from the heat and let cool to lukewarm. In batches, with the lid ajar to allow any steam to escape, purée the berry mixture in a blender (preferably a heavy-duty blender, such as Vitamix), until very smooth. Transfer to a container with a lid, cover, and refrigerate until chilled, at least 2 hours or up to 2 days.

5. To make the corn granola: Pour enough oil to come 2 inches (5 cm) up the sides of a large, heavy saucepan and heat over high heat to 375ºF (190ºC). Line a large rimmed baking sheet (half-sheet pan) with paper towels. A handful at a time, add the corn poha (it will puff and expand dramatically) and cook, stirring once or twice, until the flakes are a light golden brown, 15 to 30 seconds. Do not overcook. Using a wire spider or slotted spoon, transfer the fried poha to the baking sheet to drain and cool.

6. Position a rack in the center of the oven and preheat the oven to 200ºF (95ºC). Line another rimmed baking sheet with parchment paper. Whisk the egg white in a large bowl until foamy. Add the brown sugar, allspice, cinnamon, and nutmeg and whisk to dissolve the sugar. Add the poha and use your hands to immediately and quickly toss the poha to coat it evenly with the spiced mixture. Spread the poha on the prepared baking sheet. Bake, stirring occasionally, until the poha is crisp and lightly glazed, about 35 minutes. Turn off the oven, prop the door ajar, and let the poha cool.

7. To serve, divide the corn custard among 6 shallow bowls, followed by dollops of the blueberry sauce. Top each with an equal amount of the fresh blueberries and a handful of the poha (you will have leftover poha). Serve immediately.

Corn poha At first glance, corn poha looks like good old American corn flakes. However, there is a big difference, as most dried poha flakes are sold uncooked and must be fried before serving. You can buy corn poha at Indian grocers.

SMORESBY

Named after Crosby Beckman, our head chef in the West Village, this dish is a play on s'mores, the dessert of which we can't get enough. As this requires fire to complete, just like s'mores around the campfire, if you don't own a kitchen torch or feel safe using one, as long as the serving vessels you are using are flameproof, you can pop them under the broiler for a few seconds to brown the marshmallow crown.

> 10 ounces (280 g) bittersweet chocolate (about 62 percent cacao),
>   coarsely chopped
> 2 large eggs, at room temperature
> 1½ cups (360 ml) heavy cream
> 1 teaspoon vanilla extract
> 1¼ cups (125 g) marshmallow cream
> ⅓ cup (30 g) finely crushed graham crackers

Special equipment: Pastry bag; ½-inch (12-mm) plain star tip, such as Ateco 865; kitchen torch

1. Pulse the chocolate and eggs in a blender, preferably a heavy-duty one, such as Vitamix, until the chocolate is finely chopped and the mixture looks well blended. Heat the cream in a small saucepan over medium-high heat until small bubbles appear around the edges. With the blender running, gradually pour the hot cream through the opening and process until the chocolate has melted and the mixture is smooth, occasionally stopping the blender to scrape down the sides with a rubber spatula, about 1 minute. Add the vanilla and process to combine.

2. Divide the chocolate mixture among four 1- to 1¼-cup (240- to 300-ml) custard cups or ramekins. Cover with plastic wrap and refrigerate until chilled and set, at least 2 hours or up to 2 days.

3. To serve, transfer the marshmallow cream to a pastry bag fitted with a ½-inch (12-mm) plain star tip, such as Ateco 865. Pipe a swirl of marshmallow cream on top of each serving. Using a kitchen torch, wave the flame about 1 inch (2.5 cm) above each swirl to lightly brown it. For each serving, sprinkle about 2 tablespoons of the graham cracker crumbs over one side of the chocolate mixture. Serve immediately.

From left to right: Love Potion (page 190),
Killer Colada (page 188), Pond Point (page 193),
Ghost Train (page 195)

CHAPTER 10

COCKTAILS

We take our cocktails as seriously as our food, and we have worked to develop a beverage program with unusual and delicious drinks. We enjoy trying new spirits, some of which are made in distilleries and breweries not far from our Clinton Hill location in Brooklyn. This sense of exploration and discovery is continued in the drinks we have chosen to share with you in this chapter. We like offering cocktails that are fun and pair well with food! And just as we do with cooking ingredients, we want to open you up to some liquors that you may not have in your home bar, particularly in the realm of sweet liqueurs and bitter amari. These liquids are not just for sipping after dinner, but are also terrific as elements in some of our favorite cocktails.

A BARTENDER'S TOOLS

You need only a few tools to set up your home bar.

Cocktail shaker: We prefer a two-part Boston shaker mainly because it's sturdy and easy to clean when you're making a lot of drinks. You can also use a cobbler shaker, which has three parts, including a built-in strainer in its top part, so you won't need a separate strainer. When shaking a drink, allow a full 10 seconds' worth of agitation for thorough mixing.

Cocktail strainer: There are two kinds, which are basically interchangeable. The Hawthorne strainer has a perforated cup shape, and the julep strainer has a wire-spring rim so it fits snugly in the shaker.

Bar spoon or iced tea spoon: Not all drinks are shaken; some are stirred so aeration from shaking doesn't cloud the cocktail. When a drink calls for stirring, mix it with a long spoon for about 15 seconds to fully combine the ingredients and allow for that little bit of dilution.

Jigger: When it comes to cocktails, for precision measure by using a jigger. The most efficient ones for the home bartender hold 2 ounces (60 ml) and are marked with ½-ounce (15-ml) increments on the side.

AFTERTHOUGHT

For after work or post-meal, here is a member of the Manhattan family of cocktails, made with two amaros: Bonal, a French apéritif, and Montenegro, a popular Italian amaro.

> **2 ounces (60 ml) rye whiskey**
> **½ ounce (15 ml) Bonal**
> **½ ounce (15 ml) Montenegro**
> **3 dashes orange-flavored bitters, such as Regan's or Angostura Orange**

Stir the rye, Bonal, and Montenegro in an ice-filled shaker. Strain over an ice-filled rocks glass or into a chilled cocktail glass. Top with the bitters and serve immediately.

FANCY PHOEBE

MAKES 1 DRINK

Phoebe and her sister, Quinn, are two longtime friends of EMILY's. Since Quinn has a pizza named for her, we have honored her sister here so Phoebe has a chance to shine in cocktail format.

2 ounces (60 ml) vodka
¾ ounce (25 ml) fresh lemon juice
½ ounce (15 ml) Honey Syrup (recipe follows)
¼ ounce (10 ml) St. Elizabeth Allspice Dram

Shake the vodka, lemon juice, honey syrup, and allspice liqueur with ice to combine. Strain into an ice-filled rocks glass and serve immediately.

Honey Syrup: Shake ¼ cup (60 ml) *each* honey and very hot water in a small jar to dissolve the honey. Uncover and let cool. The syrup can be covered and refrigerated in its jar for up to 2 weeks.

FERNET ABOUT IT

MAKES 1 DRINK

Fernet Branca is another brand of the amaro/digestivo family that was originally reserved for sipping after dinner to help folks digest a meal. It has become increasingly popular as a cocktail component and serves us well in this simple drink that highlights its flavor.

> 2½ ounces (75 ml) rye whiskey
> 1 ounce (30 ml) sweet vermouth, such as Dolin
> ½ ounce (15 ml) Fernet Branca

Shake the rye, vermouth, and Fernet Branca in an ice-filled shaker. Strain into a chilled cocktail glass and serve immediately.

KILLER COLADA

MAKES 1 DRINK

We both love tropical drinks, but they're an obsession with Matt, who likes few things better than hanging out by a pool with a piña colada (or two) nearby. This might be the best colada you will ever have, with a couple of rums mashing up in a drink that goes down very easily.

> **2 ounces (60 ml) pineapple juice**
> **1½ ounces (45 ml) cream of coconut, such as Coco Lopez**
> **½ ounce (15 ml) dark rum**
> **½ ounce (15 ml) light (silver) rum**
> **½ ounce (15 ml) fresh orange juice**
> **Fresh nutmeg, for garnish**

Shake the pineapple juice, cream of coconut, dark and light rums, and orange juice in a cocktail shaker (without ice) to combine. Add ice and shake again. Strain over a single large ice cube in a rocks glass. Grate a few shavings of nutmeg over the top and serve immediately.

LOST WEEKEND

Have too many of these on Saturday night, and you will end up on your couch all Sunday. And there goes the weekend. This drink is a great chance to make your own homemade infused tequila.

> **2 ounces (60 ml) Jalapeño-Infused Tequila (recipe follows)**
> **1 ounce (30 ml) fresh Tomatillo Purée (recipe follows)**
> **¾ ounce (25 ml) fresh lime juice**
> **½ ounce (15 ml) Simple Syrup (page 190)**

Combine the jalapeño tequila, tomatillo purée, lime juice, and syrup in the glass container of a Boston shaker and add ice. Pour the mixture, including the ice, back and forth between the glass and the metal container of the shaker to combine. Strain into an ice-filled rocks glass and serve immediately.

Tomatillo Purée: Husk, rinse, and coarsely chop 1 large tomatillo. Purée in a blender.

Jalapeño-Infused Tequila: Mix 1 cup (240 ml) tequila with 4 slices of a jalapeño (do not remove the seeds) in a small jar. Cover and refrigerate for 2 days. Discard the jalapeño. The tequila can be refrigerated for up to 2 months.

LOVE POTION

Tessa Skara, our first employee ever and another resident comedian, loves Campari and built this drink for our first summer season. It's a quick and easy drink that makes a great combination to sip on.

1 ounce (30 ml) Campari
1 ounce (30 ml) fresh lemon juice
Splash of Simple Syrup (recipe follows)
Sparkling water
Lemon zest twist, for garnish

Shake the Campari, lemon juice, and syrup with ice to combine. Strain into an ice-filled wineglass and top with sparking water. Add the lemon twist and serve immediately

Simple Syrup: Shake ¼ cup (50 g) sugar with ¼ cup (60 ml) hot water in a small jar to dissolve the sugar. Uncover and let cool. The syrup can be covered and refrigerated in its jar for up to 2 weeks.

SANGRIA BLANCA

Sangria does not have to be made with red wine and berries, even though that may be the most common recipe. Here is an absolutely delicious white version that starts with a semidry Riesling, mixed with the unexpected flavors of pineapple and apple. Make a big pitcher of it, if you prefer.

> 2½ ounces (75 ml) pineapple juice
> 2 ounces (60 ml) Riesling
> 1 ounce (30 ml) apple brandy or applejack
> Simple Syrup (opposite page)

Stir the pineapple juice, Riesling, apple brandy, and syrup in an ice-filled shaker. Strain into an ice-filled wineglass and serve immediately.

POND POINT

This is a favorite drink that recalls our family summer vacations in Westhampton. With iced tea as a key ingredient, it brings back memories of backyard barbecues on warm summer nights.

2 ounces (60 ml) bourbon
¾ ounce (25 ml) Lillet Blonde
½ ounce (15 ml) Sweet Tea (recipe follows)
3 dashes Angostura bitters
Orange zest twist, for garnish

Stir the bourbon, Lillet, sweet tea, and bitters in an ice-filled shaker. Strain into a chilled cocktail glass. Twist the orange zest over the top, rub it around the rim, and serve immediately. This drink is also lovely served on the rocks.

Sweet Tea: Combine ¾ cup (180 ml) cool tap water and 1 rounded teaspoon sugar (preferably bartender's or superfine) in a small jar. Cover and shake to dissolve the sugar. Add 1 tea bag (orange pekoe or black tea) and shake again. Cover and refrigerate for 2 to 3 hours. Remove the tea bag, squeezing the tea from the bag into the jar. (Leftover tea can be covered and refrigerated for up to 2 days; serve over ice.)

FLORAL PRINT

MAKES 1 DRINK

Jake Cohen, who worked at the original EMILY, created this drink that is a fan favorite. Because of the herbaceous quality of gin, we find this combination works well as the drink is balanced with lemon and lime juice and finished with more floral flavor in the guise of a rosewater spritz. This cocktail is double-strained, which removes the fine ice flecks and foam that result from shaking.

1½ ounces (45 ml) gin
¾ ounce (25 ml) Simple Syrup (page 190)
½ ounce (15 ml) elderflower liqueur, preferably St. Germain
½ ounce (15 ml) fresh lemon juice
½ ounce (15 ml) fresh lime juice
Rosewater, in a small spray bottle

1. Shake the gin, syrup, elderflower liqueur, lemon juice, and lime juice in an ice-filled shaker.

2. Top the shaker with a Hawthorne or julep strainer and hold the strainer in place with one hand. Hold a medium-mesh wire sieve over a chilled cocktail glass in the other hand. Strain the contents of the shaker through the sieve into the glass. Lightly spray rosewater over the cocktail and serve immediately.

GHOST TRAIN

MAKES 1 DRINK

The G subway line is the one nearest to our Fulton Street restaurant and many of our staff might feel like they live on that train. Here's a smoky variation on the margarita theme that will send them on their way home in style.

1½ ounces (45 ml) mezcal
1 ounce (30 ml) ginger liqueur, preferably Canton
1 ounce (30 ml) fresh lime juice
½ ounce (15 ml) fresh grapefruit juice
Sparkling water, to finish
Fresh mint sprig, for garnish

Shake the mezcal, ginger liqueur, lime juice, and grapefruit juice in a cocktail shaker with ice. Strain into an ice-filled rocks glass. Top off with a splash of sparkling water. Garnish with the mint and serve immediately.

CHAPTER 11

SAUCES, CONDIMENTS, AND MORE

Like many restaurants, our refrigerators are stuffed with containers of the building blocks to our dishes. These flavor-packed sauces, condiments, and add-ons are not incidentals! What would the EMMY Burger or our chicken wings be without the hot-sweet concoction we lovingly call Nguyen Sauce? Our ranch dressing is much more than a salad dressing, and we're often asked to deliver a side of it to a table so the guests can dip their pizza crusts into it. They must have seen Emily do this at the bar. All sandwiches, and not just the ones we serve at the restaurants, are better when topped with a heap of caramelized onions. In a home kitchen, you'll be happy to have these extras on hand to bring an added level to your everyday cooking. Many of these can be refrigerated for quite a long time. We've also included two very special recipes for fresh ricotta cheese and pretzel buns.

Clockwise from top:
Truffle-Honey Mustard Dressing (page 28),
Pickled Jalapeños (page 209),
Fresh Ricotta (page 208), EMMY Sauce (page 125),
Nguyen Sauce (page 198), Sichuan Oil (page 200),
Aïoli (page 201), Caramelized Onions (page 206),
Chive Ranch Dressing (page 199)

NGUYEN SAUCE

Diners have Tim Nguyen to thank for this sauce that makes everyone salivate. Tim was another inaugural staff member who showed up a few weeks before the opening when we were incredibly behind on everything, and offered up his assistance. He hung hooks under the bar, drilled the legs into the tables (some of which are still crooked to this day), and then joined Matt in the kitchen to stretch dough. Matt encouraged him to play with a sauce for chicken wings, and Tim began a serious culinary journey that resulted in this incredible savory sauce that brings sweetness, tartness, heat, and garlic together in a beautiful combination. Mixed with mayo, it becomes EMMY Sauce. While this is our secret sauce for the EMMY Burger (page 125), it's also a fine dip for vegetables or chips. Tim's creation balances heady, spicy gochujang with sweet sugar and tart vinegar, and then adds mellow butter and a good dose of garlic.

⅓ cup (65 g) sugar
¼ cup (60 ml) unseasoned rice wine vinegar
½ cup (150 g) gochujang (Korean fermented chili paste)
4 tablespoons (55 g) unsalted butter
1 tablespoon (15 g) minced garlic, about 5 cloves
1 teaspoon sesame seeds
1 teaspoon black sesame seeds

Whisk the sugar and vinegar together in a medium bowl to dissolve the sugar. Add the gochujang and whisk to combine. Melt the butter in a small skillet over medium heat. Add the garlic, sesame seeds, and black sesame seeds and cook, stirring often, until the garlic is tender and fragrant but not browned, about 1½ minutes. Add to the gochujang mixture and whisk to combine. (The sauce can be covered and refrigerated for up to 1 day. Remove from the refrigerator about 1 hour before using so it's not cold when served with hot food.)

CHIVE RANCH DRESSING

MAKES ABOUT 1⅓ CUPS (315 ML)

It's probably safe to say that everyone loves creamy ranch dressing, or at least when it is as good as our homemade version. This dressing is a pale herbaceous green from the oniony chives, and it's miles away from the bottled versions you might pick up at the supermarket. Of course, it's terrific on crisp salad leaves, but we are truly addicted to it as a dip for pizza crusts.

> ¼ cup (60 ml) buttermilk
> 2 garlic cloves, minced
> 1 teaspoon coarsely ground black pepper
> 3 tablespoons finely chopped fresh chives
> 1 tablespoon finely chopped fresh mint
> 1 cup (240 ml) store-bought mayonnaise, preferably Hellmann's
> Kosher salt, to taste

Process the buttermilk, garlic, pepper, chives, and mint together in a mini food processor or a blender until the herbs are minced and the mixture turns pale green. Scrape the herb mixture into a lidded container. Add the mayonnaise and whisk well. Season to taste with salt. Transfer to a lidded container, cover, and refrigerate for up to 3 days.

SICHUAN OIL

MAKES ABOUT 1 CUP (240 ML)

With its appetizing deep red color, this versatile oil will add a heavy-duty zap of heat to many dishes. It was inspired by the hot oil condiment at Colony Grill in Stamford, Connecticut, a place that is a part of Matt's pizza DNA. We especially love it as a drizzle on pizza, but you may find it turning into your all-purpose hot sauce to sprinkle on an array of dishes.

> 1 tablespoon Sichuan peppercorns
> ½ teaspoon black peppercorns
> 1 cup (240 ml) canola or rice bran oil
> 1 tablespoon plus 2 teaspoons fine Korean chili powder
> 1 tablespoon coarse Korean chili flakes

1. Coarsely grind the Sichuan and black peppercorns together in an electric spice or coffee grinder. Combine with the oil, chili powder, and chili flakes in a small saucepan. Warm over medium-low heat until the mixture just begins to foam. Reduce the heat to very low and cook at a very low simmer to blend the flavors for about 5 minutes. Remove from the heat and let cool completely.

2. Pour the oil with all of the solids into a glass jar and cover. Store in the refrigerator for up to 2 weeks. Stir well before using.

KOREAN CHILI FLAKES AND POWDER

Korean chili flakes and chili powder are easily found at your local Asian market. Note that both the flakes and the powder may be labeled *gochugaru* or Korean chili powder, but look carefully to see the difference. Korean chili flakes are quite coarse and usually reserved for homemade kimchi. The finely ground powder is more of a seasoning, like cayenne pepper.

AÏOLI

Aïoli is the cornerstone of condiments and a simple way to enrich the flavor of many dishes. It is essentially mayonnaise and can be blended with many sauce bases to create creamier versions. In our opinion, and above all else, aïoli is the perfect dipping sauce for french fries. Here are some pointers for building a delicious aïoli:

- It is very important that the egg yolks are at room temperature. You can always just leave the whole, uncracked eggs out of the refrigerator for a couple of hours.
- While you will see recipes that use olive oil, Matt finds that gives a heavy-tasting result, and that neutral, light-bodied canola oil works better.
- There are many ways to make aïoli, but the food processor method is the easiest and is virtually foolproof. Remember that it is imperative to add the oil *slowly*.

2 large egg yolks, at room temperature
1 tablespoon rice vinegar
1 tablespoon fresh lemon juice
2 garlic cloves, crushed and peeled
½ teaspoon Dijon mustard
½ teaspoon whole grain mustard
½ teaspoon kosher salt
2 cups (480 ml) canola oil
Freshly ground black pepper

1. Add the yolks, vinegar, lemon juice, garlic, mustards, and salt into the food processor and then turn it on. One teaspoon at a time, drizzle the oil through the opening. The oil addition should take about 2 minutes, so don't rush it. Season to taste with the pepper.

2. Transfer to a lidded container. Cover and refrigerate for up to 5 days.

XIANNAISE

This is a mayonnaise named for the interplay of the French and Chinese place names *Dijon* and *Xian* in the Duck Confit Sandwich on page 146. In addition to topping sandwiches, it makes a great dip for a selection of crudités.

1 tablespoon Chinese mustard powder
1½ tablespoons water
¾ cup (180 ml) mayonnaise, preferably Kewpie
2 tablespoons hoisin sauce
2 teaspoons Sichuan Oil (page 200)

1. Stir the mustard powder and water in a custard cup or ramekin until smooth. Let stand, uncovered, for about 10 minutes for the flavor to develop.

2. Transfer the mustard mixture to a small bowl. Add the mayonnaise, hoisin sauce, and Sichuan oil and whisk until combined. Let stand for about 30 minutes before using. (Xiannaise can be refrigerated in a covered container for up to 1 week.)

MISO QUESO

Here is another sauce that we developed as a pizza topping, but it was so tasty it took on a life of its own. Try it as a warm dip for tortilla chips, and you'll see what we mean. We use American cheese because, as hard as we have tried, we just can't find another variety that melts so smoothly.

⅓ cup (75 ml) heavy cream
⅓ cup (75 ml) whole milk
2 tablespoons ssamjang
8 ounces (225 g) diced white American cheese (about 2½ cups)
Freshly ground black pepper

Heat the cream, milk, and ssamjang in a medium saucepan over medium heat, whisking to dissolve the miso. Reduce the heat to very low. Gradually whisk in the cheese, making sure that the first addition has melted before adding another. Season to taste with pepper. Serve warm. (The miso queso can be cooled, transferred to a lidded container, covered, and refrigerated for up to 5 days. Reheat gently in a small saucepan over low heat, or on medium power in a microwave oven, stirring occasionally until hot and smooth.)

SCALLION KIMCHI

MAKES ABOUT 2 CUPS (480 ML); 6 TO 8 SERVINGS

Kimchi made with napa cabbage is most well known, but we like this scallion kimchi as a topping for the Lammy Burger (page 134) and The Pig Freaker pizza (page 113); it's also good to have around for adding to other dishes as you may see fit like a Sunday morning omelette that needs a little boost! Allow at least 4 days for the kimchi to ferment at room temperature before using. Use a glass baking dish to make this so you can easily detect the bubbling signs of fermentation.

8 ounces (225 g) scallions
¼ cup (60 ml) gochujang (Korean fermented chili paste)
⅓ cup (50 g) finely chopped garlic
2½ tablespoons soy sauce
2½ tablespoons sugar
2 teaspoons kosher salt

1. Trim the root end from the scallions and cut them, top to bottom, into 2-inch (5-cm) lengths. Whisk the gochujang, garlic, soy sauce, sugar, and salt together in a small bowl. Layer the scallions in an 8-inch (20-cm) glass or ceramic baking dish, using a silicone spatula to spread them with the gochujang mixture. Cover with two layers of plastic wrap. Lightly crush the scallions through the plastic with your fingertips to release some of the scallion juices. Top with a second baking dish. Place a heavy can in the baking dish to weigh it down slightly.

2. Let stand at room temperature until tiny bubbles are visible in the dish, 3 to 5 days, depending on the ambient temperature and the amount of wild yeasts you have in your kitchen. Be sure the scallions are covered with juice, and press down on the scallions to release more juice.

3. Transfer the kimchi and all juices to a lidded container, cover tightly, and refrigerate for at least 1 day or up to 2 weeks. As the kimchi ages and ferments more, its flavor and aroma will increase. You can pop the lid occasionally to let any built-up gases escape. Let it ferment to the level of funkiness you like.

Clockwise from top:
Nguyen Sauce (page 198),
Scallion Kimchi (page 204), Sichuan Oil (page 200),
Chive Ranch Dressing (page 199)

CARAMELIZED ONIONS

MAKES ABOUT 1½ CUPS (360 G)

It's hard for us to imagine cooking without caramelized onions, which are featured on the EMMY Burger (page 125). Caramelized onions are fairly easy to make. We like them because they are rich, sweet, and add an abundance of flavor to everything they are paired with. This is another recipe that you can store leftovers of in the fridge to use as creative additions in your everyday cooking. Perhaps try garnishing a white pizza with this delectable topping as you create and explore.

> 2 tablespoons unsalted butter
> 3 large yellow onions, about 2¼ pounds (1 kg) total, cut into
>   ¼-inch (6-mm) half-moons
> Kosher salt and freshly ground black pepper

1. Heat the butter in a large nonstick skillet over medium-high heat. Add the onions and season lightly with salt and pepper. Cook, stirring occasionally and separating the onion layers, until the onions wilt, about 5 minutes.

2. Reduce the heat to medium-low. Cook, stirring occasionally, until the onions are very tender and a deep beige, 30 to 40 minutes. Adjust the heat as needed so they cook steadily without browning or crisping around the edges. Serve warm or cool to room temperature. The onions can be covered and refrigerated for up to 5 days. Let stand at room temperature for about 30 minutes before using.

GARLIC CONFIT AND GARLIC OIL

MAKES ABOUT 1 CUP (240 ML) *EACH* CONFIT AND OIL

When raw garlic cloves are slowly cooked in oil, they mellow into a golden and tender version of themselves that we use in many dishes at EMILY. When making this oil and confit, you will create two great condiments that can be used in dressings, sauces, and more.

> **2 large, firm heads garlic**
> **1 cup (240 ml) canola oil**

1. Using a sharp knife, peel each garlic clove, keeping it intact—do not smash the garlic to loosen the peel.

2. Put the garlic in a large saucepan and add enough oil to cover it by about ½ inch (12 mm). Heat over medium heat just until tiny bubbles start to form around the garlic cloves. Reduce the heat to very low. Cook, uncovered, without stirring, just until the garlic turns a darker shade of beige and is tender, about 1 hour. Remove from the heat and let the garlic cool in the oil for 1 to 2 hours.

3. Using a wire spider or a slotted spoon, carefully transfer the garlic to a lidded container. Pour enough of the oil over the garlic to cover the cloves, reserving the remaining oil for another use. Strain the garlic oil through a fine-mesh wire sieve into another lidded container. Cover the confit and oil and refrigerate for up to 1 month.

FRESH RICOTTA

MAKES 2 CUPS (455 G)

Fresh ricotta is an item we choose to make from scratch at the restaurants because the difference between homemade and store-bought is stark. And, fresh ricotta is surprisingly easy and fun to make, so give it a try at home! Many cooks like to reuse the whey for other kitchen jobs like making bread and cooking vegetables and as an ingredient in fermented foods like sauerkraut.

2 quarts (2 L) organic whole milk
2 teaspoons kosher salt
¼ cup (60 ml) fresh lemon juice
1 tablespoon red wine vinegar
½ cup (120 ml) heavy cream

Special equipment: Cheesecloth

1. Heat the milk in a large nonreactive saucepan over medium heat, stirring almost constantly to discourage scalding (especially on the bottom), until it reaches 195ºF (90ºC) on an instant-read thermometer. This will take about 10 minutes. Remove from the heat. Whisk in the salt.

2. Stir in the lemon juice and vinegar. Let stand until the mixture has semi-solid curds floating on top of a thin, cloudy liquid (the whey), 10 to 15 minutes.

3. Line a large wire sieve with a double thickness of rinsed and wrung cheesecloth and suspend the sieve over a large bowl. Using a wire spider or a slotted spoon, transfer the curds to the cheesecloth, discarding the bulk of the whey as it gathers in the bowl, or reserve the whey for another use (see headnote). Fold any excess cheesecloth over onto the curds and place a saucer on top. Let the curds drain for about 45 minutes, or until you have about 1½ cups (325 g) of drained, fairly dry curds in the cheesecloth.

4. Transfer the curds to a medium bowl, reserving the drained whey. Gradually stir in the cream to enrich the ricotta. If the ricotta is still too dry for your taste, stir in as much of the reserved whey as you wish. Cover and refrigerate until chilled and set, at least 2 hours or overnight. The ricotta can be refrigerated for up to 2 days.

PICKLED JALAPEÑOS

MAKES ABOUT 1 CUP (150 G)

Another surprisingly easy-to-make condiment—you'll have a big batch of sliced chiles ready to be pulled into action, and the exact yield depends on the size of the jalapeños.

4 large jalapeños
1 cup (240 ml) rice vinegar, as needed

Special equipment: Two-cup (480-ml) lidded jar

1. Cut off and discard the jalapeño stems. Slice the jalapeños crosswise into rounds about ⅛-inch (3-mm) thick. Do not remove the seeds. Transfer the jalapeños to a 2-cup (480-ml) lidded jar.

2. Bring the vinegar to a boil in a small nonreactive saucepan over high heat. Pour the hot vinegar into the jar. Add more vinegar as needed to cover the jalapeños. Let cool, uncovered.

3. Cover the jar and refrigerate for at least 1 day before using. The jalapeños can be stored in the refrigerator for up to 3 months.

PRETZEL BUNS

MAKES 6 ROLLS

We purchase our pretzel buns from one of New York's favorite bread makers, Tom Cat Bakery. If you don't have a similar bakery to source them near you, here is our recipe for a homemade version of the rolls. Pretzel buns are the only kind of bun we personally serve our sandwiches on, burgers or otherwise. And, one of our favorite pastimes is making these rolls together at home—so roll up your sleeves and make them with someone you love.

¼ cup (60 ml) warm (105º to 115ºF/40º to 45ºC) water
One ¼-ounce (7-g) envelope active dry yeast, about 2¼ teaspoons
3 tablespoons light brown sugar
¾ cup (180 ml) cold water
⅓ cup (75 ml) whole milk
2 tablespoons unsalted butter, melted
3¾ cups (485 g) bread flour, as needed
3 tablespoons whole-wheat flour
3 tablespoons rye flour
2 teaspoons kosher salt
Vegetable oil, for the bowl
½ cup (125 g) baking soda
Pretzel salt, for sprinkling (optional)

1. To make the dough in a heavy-duty mixer: Pour the warm water into the bowl of a standing heavy-duty mixer. Sprinkle in the yeast, add ½ teaspoon of the brown sugar, and let stand until you see some bubbling or foaming in the mixture, 5 to 10 minutes. Stir to dissolve the yeast. Add the cold water, milk, butter, and remaining brown sugar. Add the bread, whole-wheat, and rye flours with the salt. Attach the bowl to the mixer and affix the dough hook. Mix on medium-low speed until the mixture forms a soft, sticky dough that cleans the sides of the bowl. Turn off the mixer and cover the top of the bowl with a kitchen towel. Let stand for 10 minutes. Knead on medium-low speed until the dough is smooth but soft and tacky to the touch, about 8 minutes.

To make the dough by hand: Pour the warm water into a large bowl, sprinkle in the yeast with ½ teaspoon of the brown sugar, and let stand for 5 minutes. Stir to dissolve the yeast. Add the cold water, milk, butter, and remaining brown sugar. Stir in 1 cup (140 g) bread flour with the whole-wheat flour, rye flour, and salt. Gradually stir in enough bread flour to make a dough that you cannot stir. Turn out onto a floured work surface and knead, adding more flour as needed, to make a smooth, slightly sticky dough, 8 to 10 minutes. The dough is supposed to feel tacky, so don't add too much flour.

2. Lightly oil a medium bowl. Turn out the dough onto a floured work surface and shape into a ball; place in the bowl, smooth side down. Turn over so the smooth side is up and lightly coated with oil. Cover tightly with plastic wrap and let stand in a warm place until doubled, 1 to 1¼ hours. (Or refrigerate for at least 8 or up to 24 hours.)

3. Line a large rimmed baking sheet (half-sheet pan) with parchment paper. Turn out the dough onto an unfloured work surface and knead briefly to deflate the dough. Cut the dough into 6 equal portions. (For the best results, weigh each portion on a kitchen scale; each should weigh about 150 g.) One at a time, shape each portion into a taut ball by tucking the sides of the dough to meet underneath the ball. Place the balls, smooth side up, about 2 inches (5 cm) apart on the prepared baking sheet. Cover loosely with plastic wrap and let stand in a warm place until almost doubled in volume, about 45 minutes. (If the dough is chilled, this will take about 2 hours.)

4. Position a rack in the center of the oven and preheat to 425ºF (220ºC). Line another rimmed baking sheet with parchment paper. Place a lint-free kitchen towel near the stove.

5. Bring 4 quarts (3.8 L) water to a boil in a large nonaluminum pot. Gradually stir in the baking soda—it will foam. Two at a time, carefully add the rolls to the water and cook, turning once, until the dough surface looks set, about 30 seconds per side. Using a wire spider or a slotted spoon, transfer the rolls, bottom side down, to the towel and drain for a few seconds. Transfer the rolls to the second parchment-lined pan, spacing them well apart. If desired, sprinkle the wet tops with pretzel salt.

6. Using kitchen scissors, snip an X about 1½ inches (4 cm) wide in the top of each ball. Bake until the rolls are deeply browned, 18 to 20 minutes. Let cool on the pan for about 3 minutes. Transfer the rolls to a wire rack and let cool completely. (The rolls are best the day they are baked. Leftovers can be stored in an airtight container at room temperature for up to 1 day. Before serving, wrap in aluminum foil and bake in a preheated 350ºF/180ºC oven until heated, 15 to 20 minutes.)

ACKNOWLEDGMENTS

We are truly grateful to the many incredible people who have supported us through the process of turning our dream into a reality—there are too many of you to name individually; please know if you are not mentioned directly, you are in our hearts and we are thankful.

And while we mention many staff members in the text of this book, we are grateful to every single hardworking, loyal, and dedicated person in our employ who helps keep our vision alive.

We want to thank Jim Lahey and Ken Forkish for the inspiration we garnered from their cookbooks early on as we developed our dough. A warm thank-you to our friend Adam Kuban for pizza and burger testing and advice over the years.

Thank you to the food community that has become a network of support, learning, and friendship for Matt, and thank you to the yoga community that has helped Emily maintain perspective, balance, and breath.

Thank you to the neighborhood regulars who have become the bedrock of our community and have turned into true friends and family.

We extend thanks to our growth partners, Howard Greenstone and Ken Levitan, who have helped us take the step from being a small mom-and-pop to spreading our pizza love everywhere!

Thank you, Rick Rodgers, for helping us navigate this intense process of writing a book and thank you to Pamela Cannon and the entire Penguin Random House organization for bringing this cookbook to life. Thank you to Evan Sung for his talent behind the camera and to David Vigliano for putting these wheels into motion.

To everyone who has touched our lives over the past five years, thank you. Every guest, instagrammer, blogger, excited fan, reviewer, and writer who has supported us, thank you, thank you.

Thank you to Rafael Vasquez for believing in us since day one, and for helping us build the original location without question. And above all, it goes without saying, we would not be here without the love, support, patience, advice, and hugs of Rex, Rona, and Lauren Shaw, and Angela, Tom, Christa, and William Hyland. We love you all so much.

INDEX